My Divine Connection with God

A Devotional

Meditations of the Heart

CAROLYN CROW

CROSSBOOKS

CrossBooks™
A Division of LifeWay
1663 Liberty Drive
Bloomington, IN 47403
www.crossbooks.com
Phone: 1-866-879-0502

Scripture taken from the King James Version of the Bible.

All Scripture quotations in this publications are from The Message. Copyright © by
Eugene H. Peterson 1993, 1994, 1995, 1996, 2000, 2001, 2002. Used by permission of
NavPress Publishing Group.

Scripture taken from the Holy Bible, NEW INTERNATIONAL VERSION®.
Copyright © 1973, 1978, 1984 by Biblica, Inc. All rights reserved worldwide. Used
by permission. NEW INTERNATIONAL VERSION® and NIV® are registered
trademarks of Biblica, Inc. Use of either trademark for the offering of goods or services
requires the prior written consent of Biblica US, Inc.

Scripture quotations taken from the Holy Bible, New Living Translation,
Copyright © 1996, 2004. Used by permission of Tyndale House
Publishers, Inc., Wheaton, Illinois 60189. All rights reserved.

Scripture taken from the Holman Christian Standard Bible ® Copyright © 2003, 2002,
2000, 1999 by Holman Bible Publishers. All rights reserved.

Scripture quotations are from The Holy Bible, English Standard Version® (ESV®),
copyright © 2001 by Crossway, a publishing ministry of Good News Publishers. Used
by permission. All rights reserved.

Scripture quotations taken from the New American Standard Bible®, Copyright © 1960,
1962, 1963, 1968, 1971, 1972, 1973, 1975, 1977, 1995 by The Lockman Foundation. Used
by permission. (www.Lockman.org)

First published by CrossBooks   04/25/2014

ISBN: 978-1-4627-3707-9 (sc)
ISBN: 978-1-4627-3708-6 (hc)
ISBN: 978-1-4627-3706-2 (e)

Library of Congress Control Number: 2014907822

Printed in the United States of America.

This book is printed on acid-free paper.

Any people depicted in stock imagery provided by Thinkstock are models,
and such images are being used for illustrative purposes only.

Certain stock imagery © Thinkstock.

Contents

Dedication

Affectionately dedicated to the life and legacy of Pastor Joe Keith Crow, my beloved late husband, who made his transition to eternity on October 28, 2011.

Also to my beloved children, Travonn Crow and Ebonee Crow-Cole (Calvin).

Acknowledgments

I sincerely appreciate my many friends and family members who have been my greatest supporters during the process of my writing. Your encouragement kept me on task during those challenging times when I thought nothing else was left in me. I am thankful to Carolyn Bell and Eunice V. Akoto for their editorial comments. I am especially thankful to Carolyn, who walked alongside me during the course of this journey. Your friendship is priceless.

I am also indebted to my two children, Travonn and Ebonee, who stuck with me while accomplishing this milestone. You are forever loved and greatly appreciated. Above all, I am eternally grateful to my heavenly Father, who graced me with His wisdom and guidance during the entire process. Without Him, this book would not have been possible.

Praises for My Divine Connection with God

Divine connections with God so often go undetected. Many pass them off without a second thought. Author Carolyn Crow is not part of the many. Her life's journey has caused her to walk in dark valleys, but in those times, she learned to treasure those divine connections. Carolyn is a gifted writer and communicator that uplifts and encourages the reader. Her stories easily become the reader's story. You are going to find yourself reading familiar moments in this book, because they are so like yours. You are going to find, as Carolyn has, that the path is not new to humankind, but the journey has been marked out by other travelers. The apostle Paul refers to life's tough moments as *common to man*. Life's tough moments are more manageable when we realize there are others walking near.

It is my joy to be Carolyn's pastor. Her love for God and others is evident in all that she is. She is truly a blessing to everyone she encounters. As you read this book, I pray you too will have a divine connection with our heavenly Father.

Rev. Rick Mays
Lead pastor, Trinity Temple Assembly of God

In this book, the author Carolyn Crow shares both her struggles and her joy. She also provides valuable lessons that challenge you to remain faithful to God when facing life's circumstances. I thank God for the wisdom and insight that He has given her. The work that she has done throughout the pages of *My Divine Connection with God* is timely, appropriate, and highly spiritual. I pray that every reader will be inspired, motivated, and challenged to grow to a higher level of maturity in their daily and personal walk with God.

Rev. James H. Giles, Sr.
Presiding Elder, African Methodist Episcopal Church

Relying on God's grace, Carolyn learned much through the season of grief and loss. In this book of devotionals, she shares with us how to use God's Word to overcome and grow from life's disappointments and pain. Her message of hope and redemption through Jesus Christ will inspire and encourage you to live joyfully through life's most difficult challenges.

Sarah Teed
Attorney-at-law

It is our privilege to know Carolyn as a dear friend for many years. As we labored together in ministry along with her husband, the late Pastor Joe Crow, he always encouraged her to write and pursue her passion. As a woman of prayer and strong in faith, we believed that God has raised her up to bring a message of faith and hope to this modern generation. *My Divine Connection with God* will give you deep insight on the struggles, the pain, the joy, and the victories that Carolyn experienced during the illness and transition of her husband. In the midst of his illness, Carolyn continued to write and publish articles of hope. This book will bring hope to people of all walks of life. The Bible says,

> We do not lose heart. Though outwardly we are wasting away, yet inwardly we are being renewed day by day. For our light and momentary troubles are achieving for us an eternal glory that far outweighs them all. So we fix our eyes not on what is seen, but on what is unseen. For what is seen is temporary, but what is unseen is eternal.
>
> 2 Corinthians 4:16–18 (NIV)

James and Donnetta Frierson
Pastors of New Life Christian Fellowship

Preface

This has been one of the most challenging yet rewarding tasks that I have ever been assigned to carry out. My mandate to write this book of devotionals came in the prime of my life and ministry, when medical reports indicated that my husband was suffering from bladder cancer.

Needless to say, I stumbled my way onto a dark and dreary journey that I was not familiar with. On this journey, I divinely connected with God while pouring out my soul to Him. And out of my outpour, *My Divine Connection with God* was born. During this season, my faith was truly tested. There were times I questioned my own survival. By God's grace, I survived, and I became more determined to use every test and trial to help bless the lives of others.

As I open to you the chambers of my heart, I begin with a narration of the "Unexpected Journey" from the time of Joe's diagnosis to the time he transitioned into glory. Thereafter, you will find a series of devotionals that highlight some of my up-and-down moments and how God sustained me during this tragic experience. As each devotional unfolds, it shows proof that God's healing power is still evident among His people. I pray that every word written will bring healing and encouragement to your souls and help you realize that God will never allow you to walk your journey alone.

It has often been said that those who once needed encouragement ended up reaching out and inspiring others. Therefore, I pray that everyone who reads this book will extend themselves to others who are in need of encouragement. That has been my motivation for writing this book.

Part 1

The Unexpected Journey

It was late January 2009. Joe was sound asleep, recovering from the simple procedure that would determine our next step. As I patiently waited for him to awaken, a voice from the intercom called my name. "Please report to the consultation room." The doctor met me with a joyful and blissful smile as I approached him. He handled himself quite well as he began explaining the analysis of the test.

"The good news is," he began, "his left kidney looks normal, but there is a mass attached to his right kidney, which is abnormal. I believe it to be cancer."

You can only imagine what my heart felt after receiving this news. This unexpected announcement knocked the breath right out of me. It was certainly a blow that I wasn't prepared for. I tried very hard to remain in control, but from within, I could feel my emotions churning. They were rolling over me like the swells of the rising tide. I was baffled, confused, and unsure of what to do next.

This isn't what I expected, I thought as I reached for my belongings and headed to the hospital parking lot. I didn't know where I was going; I just needed to get away. The more I walked, the more confused I became. Beads of moisture began to gather in the corners of my eyes. The moisture turned to tears, and I started feeling completely incompetent. "Oh, help me, Lord," I cried. It took all my might to remain steady, just to keep from lowering my body to the ground. I had never felt so helpless in my life. I wanted to run to the depths of the earth, screaming as loudly as I could in order to get it all out. If it were possible, I would have run out of the world without returning. "God, where are you in the midst of this?" I kept asking.

> Be strong and of good courage; be not
> frightened, neither be dismayed; for the Lord
> your God is with you wherever you go.
> Joshua 1:9 (NLT)

Despite my feelings, I knew I had to get it together. At that point, Joe had not been told the devastating news. He was a man of faith. He preached and taught the word of faith, but I wondered what his initial reaction was going to be. Once he was told, I never saw him waver. He was more determined to fight for his faith than ever before. Throughout the years of his ministry, his favorite quote came from Romans 10:8. (NASB) "But what does it say? The word is near you, in your mouth and in your heart." That is, the word of faith which we are preaching.

In the midst of the storms of life, it can be difficult to believe anything good will come. But it will. Sometimes, it takes awhile to see what God is doing. However, if we choose to believe that He is orchestrating the final outcome for good, that belief can provide the motivation we need to persevere in the face of the unexpected.

Fighting with Zeal

Joe's first diagnosis was a malignancy on his right kidney. However, more tests and surgery indicated that he had aggressive bladder cancer. As we began wading through the medical reports, we came to terms with cancer as a part of our lives. We didn't know what to expect in the months ahead, but we continued with peaceful and joyful spirits, knowing very well that God was in control. We spent very little time discussing the cancer itself. Our focus was the real "C word," which is *Christ*. We didn't have time to pucker down to the Enemy. The only thing that would suffice for this battle was to gather up all the spiritual ammunition that we could in order to stay strong and fight with zeal.

> Finally, my brethren, be strong in the Lord, and in the power of his might. Put on the whole armour of God, that ye may be able to stand against the wiles of the devil. For we wrestle not against flesh and blood, but against principalities, against powers, against the rulers of the darkness of this world, against spiritual wickedness in high places. Wherefore take unto you the whole armour of God, that ye may be able to withstand in the evil day, and having done all, to stand.
> Ephesians 6:10–13

If anyone had told me a couple of years prior that Joe would be diagnosed with cancer, I would have predicted that I would have to be checked into a psych ward. I was truly amazed at the peace and contentment God gave us. We continued with life as normal while preparing to take on the next measure.

We were scheduled to meet with the oncologist, who would explain all necessary procedures and treatments, exactly two weeks later. Our first step was surgery to remove the mass from his kidney. After surgery, the pathology report revealed that he had made 80 percent recovery. At this percentage rate, we felt that we had a great chance at beating this cancer.

In the months ahead, we continued to face unfortunate situations, one after another. Then came the chemotherapy and radiation. However, the disease continued its assault.

Amazingly, I never heard Joe complain. His faith in Christ was his solid rock. He had no fear, no anger, and more profoundly, he had a deep sense that his God would sustain him. No matter how bad he felt, he continued to radiate God's unspeakable joy.

> Don't be dejected and sad, for the joy
> of the Lord is your strength!
> Nehemiah 8:10 (NLT)

A Father's Day Special

◆ ◆ ◆

Taking time for those you love is never a waste of time. However, spending time with our children was very important to us. Although they lived apart from us in different cities and states, we made it a point to have family time. On each Tuesday night at 7:30 p.m. sharp, the four of us connected three-way via phone.

The first half hour was spent catching up on life, while the last half hour was spent praying fervently for each other.

On one particular night I vividly remember the conversation that Joe had with Trey and Ebonee. He said, "I am very proud of everything you guys have accomplished, but the greatest thing I can be proud of as a father is that both of you are saved." Their sobbing hearts rejoiced during a brief moment of silence while processing the most priceless and liberating words that had ever been spoken.

My son, Trey, later explained, "I breathed a sigh of relief while losing my fight against tears." He said, "For once in my life, I felt like a hero, not from what I may have achieved through worldly possessions, but by making one simple and right choice."

> But whatever gain I had, I counted as loss for the sake of Christ. Indeed, I count everything as loss because of the surpassing worth of knowing Christ Jesus my Lord. For his sake I have suffered the loss of all things and count them as rubbish, in order that I may gain Christ.
> Philippians 3:7–8 (ESV)

Just two weeks later, a medium-sized envelope arrived in the mail. Inside the sealed envelope was an ivory-colored card that was shadowed with dark-brown leaves. It had an open message marked with gold imprint, which stood out in a bold and cursive font. It read,

> To a special dad. No one can take the place of a dad whose heart is as big as his smiles, whose advice is as great as his sense of humor, whose caring is as deep as his love of family.

Inside the card, a special message was enclosed in Trey's very own handwriting.

Just want to thank you for being the father you are to me, and giving me advice and praying for me when I wasn't praying for myself. You made me become the man that I am. I am not where I want to be, but I am not where I used to be. I thank God every day for you, because I know you had plenty of chances to run out on me, Ebonee, and Mom, but you hung in there. I know you had to have God in your life in order to listen to Mom's mouth. LOL! Thank you for being my father and my pastor.

Love you,
Travonn

As I watched my husband read the card over and over again, I knew by the look in his eyes that it was something special about this Father's Day. Just four months later, he departed from his fatherhood here in order to go and greet his heavenly Father.

We have to endeavor to make sure that our goals and accomplishments are kept in proper perspective while making Christ number one. And as we grow and mature in our Christian walk, we must realize that not all the worldly substances can stand in competition with our salvation in Christ. Let's consider Matthew 16:26, a very familiar saying of Jesus. "For what is a man profited, if he shall gain the whole world, and lose his own soul? or what shall a man give in exchange for his soul?"

The Final Days

The last days of Joe's life were more than I could bear. Unfortunately, his condition took a drastic change for the worse. I will never forget sitting at my piano, playing one of his favorite songs entitled "He Won't Fail You." He slipped in behind me and placed his chin on my shoulder. As he had always done, he started singing until his soul got happy. I could sense the tiredness in his voice as well as his body. When he eventually left the room, I noticed his steps had gotten shorter. I realized I was losing the Joe I had once known. He was disappearing right before my very eyes. Part of me wanted to believe the best, yet part of me was not willing to accept the truth.

> What do you do when you watch your loved one slowly fade away? My only option was to trust God and believe that He would get me through it.

Shortly afterward, he was lying in bed. When I entered the bedroom, I noticed his countenance conveyed God's glory. He asked, "Where are those little women that were dressed in white? They have been ministering to me." At that point, I didn't know what to think or what to say. It was after his transition when I realized those women that he was referring to were angels. I believe they were the receiving angels that were coming to take him to his heavenly home. However, they returned and received him twelve days later.

Faithfulness in the Face of Death

❖ ❖ ❖

Joe was a humorous guy. He was fun to be around and delighted in the simple pleasures of life. He also had an adventurous side of him, which came out whenever there was a catastrophe nearby. He was always ready to lend a hand and help those in need. But most importantly, he was a pillar of faith. His faith, love, and commitment for Christ were often demonstrated in remarkable ways.

Just days before his transition, he was lying in the hospital bed with his hand lifted toward heaven. At once, he started reciting this declaration of faith, which he faithfully quoted every Sunday morning before his message.

> Hold your Bibles in the air … Please repeat after me …
> This is my Bible. I am what it says that I am. I can do
> what it says I can do. It is the infallible Word of God,
> the solid rock on which I stand. Nothing can defeat me.
> I have peace, I have joy, I have everything that I need
> in Christ. Amen!

Frankly, this was a beautiful experience to behold. Even in the face of death, he proved to cling to his faith in God.

Trey was amazed at his dad's recitation. He then took a step toward the window, gazing into the clear-blue sky, with endless teardrops beating against the windowsill. At that moment, a new level of faith transpired and we had to hold on to it, no matter what our hearts were feeling.

As children of God, we may face challenges that will rock our faith, but the ultimate challenge is holding on to what we believe. That belief is our faith in God and His Word. The apostle Paul admonishes us to "Let us hold fast to the profession of our faith without wavering; for he is faithful that promised" (Hebrews 10:23).

> In the face of trouble, who are you? In the face of
> pain and struggle, who do your heart cling to?
>
> God wants you to utterly trust in Him. You have
> His Word planted on the inside of you. Hold strong
> to it and make it a part of your daily confession.
>
> My dear friend, stand firm. You can prevail
> in the face of your struggles. First John 5:4
> declares, "For whatsoever is born of God
> overcometh the world: and this is the victory
> that overcometh the world, even our faith."

Letting Go

It was only thirty minutes away from midnight on October 28, 2011. This day will forever be a marked moment in my life, being the day when my world was thrown off its axis. After nearly three years of being in this battle, Joe transitioned from this life to go and take up his permanent citizenship in eternity. I stood by his bedside and watched him slowly slip away. No matter how ill your loved one may become, you are never ready or prepared to let them go. But I had to come to grips that his life here on earth had ended, and it was time to release him back to his maker.

As I tightly held his frail hand, I whispered my very last words. "I love you, and I will always love you. You will always be my buddy boy. Don't worry about me; God will take care of me. If you are ready to go home and be with Jesus, it's okay." Then in a brief sigh of relief, he mustered up enough strength and replied, "Okay." There were no words that could justify the totality of this trauma. He was much more than my husband of thirty-one years. He was my junior high sweetheart, best friend, companion, and soul mate. He was also my pastor, my partner in ministry, my buddy, my encourager, and someone I enjoyed life with.

Nevertheless, I will forever reflect upon the good memories that he left behind with great anticipation on seeing him again. Although his transition was much sooner than I expected or wanted, he is far better off in the presence of the King of Kings, his wonderful Savior. His transition brings comfort to my heart, knowing that he will never experience the depths of despair again. "For I consider that the sufferings of this present time are not worthy to be compared with the glory which shall be revealed in us" (Romans 8:18). (NASB) "For our citizenship is in heaven; from which also we look for the Savior, the Lord Jesus Christ" (Philippians 3:20). (KJV 2000)

My faith shall remain strong as I trust God to walk with me and guide me through this season. As difficult as it is, this opens a new chapter in my life. Therefore, I must charter a new course and move on to the destination which God has chosen for me.

> May I ask, are you ready for the appointed
> day? We are told that Christ shall come in
> a moment, in a twinkling of an eye.
> 1 Corinthians 15:52

When the Bottom Falls Out

◆ ◆ ◆

After spending nearly two weeks in the hospital, it was now time to return home. However, at this time, I was returning home alone. When I took the first step inside, my heart bolted and fear crammed its way into my mind. My tears began to flow like waterfalls. I lost my balance when I noticed the empty chair that he once occupied, his side of the bed, his side of the closet filled with clothes and shoes that he would no longer wear. Never again would I hear the sounds of preparation for church on Sunday morning as he would say, "Let's hurry, baby." The disappointment was so overwhelming when I realized my house, which was once called a home, had now become an empty structure.

As I was trying to process it all, I thought at any minute I would be swallowed up by the tidal wave of grief. I wanted to scream, I wanted to call out his name, but what was the use? He couldn't answer. Seemingly, the bottom was failing out. I now realized life as I once knew it was now over. At this point, I had little hope that the sun would ever shine again.

God is faithful and He has remained steady in giving me hope, as I can now witness that the sun is beginning to peak from behind the dark clouds. Although I still cry and struggle,

I am growing and learning. I am very grateful for those special people that God has placed on my path that have encouraged and reminded me that there is a future.

> Thank you, my dear friends. You have been
> faithful to stand with me, and there is no way
> possible I would have made it without you.

In times like this, you need friends who will allow you to be honest without condemnation. Honesty has been a great part of my healing. However, the pain and sorrow that I am going through will not go wasted. I will use my experience as a conduit to help bless the lives of others. Psalm 126:6 declares, "He that goeth forth and weepeth, bearing precious seed, shall doubtless come again with rejoicing, bringing his sheaves with him."

My Aching Soul

♦ ♦ ♦

It was December 25, 2011, a cold and rainy morning in Atlanta, Georgia. My broken heart was aching due to the loss of my beloved Joe Keith just fifty-nine days earlier. I tried so hard not to reminisce on the past thirty-one Christmases. Every moment kept reminding me of the treasured memories that we once shared. Although I was blessed to be surrounded by insurmountable love and laughter, it didn't keep the heartache from penetrating my soul.

It was a hard day to push through. Eventually, I found myself leaving the room to escape from it all. Little Camryn, my six-year-old granddaughter, sensed something was wrong. Just minutes later, she approached me with her bright beautiful eyes, softly asking, "Why are you crying? You have no reason to cry about Big Poppa. He's in a better place." She took her little arms and embraced me, patting my back gently. "I'll keep my hand on your back and hold you," she declared. My tears began to multiply, but at the same time, the peace of God saturated my entire being as her tender touch made me feel as though I was in the arms of Jesus Himself.

It is very likely that almost everyone will deal with a broken heart at some point. It is during such times when God seems the most absent in our lives. We may not always feel His presence, but He is certainly with us. The words of the psalmist David solidify this. "The LORD *is* nigh unto them that are of a broken heart; and saveth such as be of a contrite spirit" (Psalm 34:18).

We may never comprehend the pain that comes from a broken heart. But we can be assured that when we hurt, God hurts also. No tear falls here on earth without God feeling the hurt in heaven. Consider the reassuring words of Psalm 30:5, where the psalmist David declares, "Weeping may endure for a night, but joy cometh in the morning."

Disappointed but Not Defeated

◆ ◆ ◆

No matter how hard we would like to avoid them, at some point, disappointments will invade our lives. But it's never to our liking. Disappointments can sometime leave us broken, confused, and vulnerable. They can even play on our emotions.

Since the passing of my beloved, the journey has not been easy. However, I am learning each day how to live by God's grace. Although I am a bit disappointed, I am not defeated. Defeat only comes to those who quit. His Word tells us that we are more than conquerors through Him that loves us. Through Him, we have the power to overcome anything that opposes our faith. After all, if God is for us, then who can stand against us?

We can look inside the life of Job, who suffered many losses. The Bible speaks of him being a blameless and upright man fearing God and turning away from evil. Job outright admits that his complaint is bitter and doesn't understand what is going on. He could have given up and quit, but still he proclaimed, "Though He slay me, yet will I trust in him" (Job 13:15).

> My beloved friends, smile big and count
> it pure joy. You may encounter many
> disappointments, but you will never be defeated
> as long as you place your trust in God.

> We are hard pressed on every side, but not crushed;
> perplexed, but not in despair; persecuted, but not
> abandoned; struck down, but not destroyed.
> 2 Corinthians 4:8–9 (NIV)

Your Reflections

_____

_____

_____

_____

_____

_____

_____

_____

_____

_____

_____

_____

_____

_____

_____

_____

_____

_____

_____

_____

_____

_____

_____

_____

_____

_____

_____

_____

_____

_____

_____

_____

_____

_____

_____

_____

_____

_____

_____

_____

_____

_____

_____

_____

_____

_____

_____

_____

_____

_____

_____

_____

_____

_____

_____

For I know the thoughts that I think toward you, saith the LORD,
thoughts of peace, and not of evil, to give you an expected end
(Jeremiah 29:11).

Part 2

It's Okay to Ask Why

◆ ◆ ◆

SOME SAY WE DON'T HAVE THE RIGHT TO QUESTION GOD, while others say, "Why not? He's our heavenly Father." You may be surprised to know that there are more Christians who are not willing to admit that they have wrestled with the question "Why, God?" As you well know, life can be puzzling sometimes, and when it doesn't make sense, our humanity seeks to understand why.

Although I am fully aware that there are some things that will remain a mystery until the end, I believe that God will not become angry with us when we go to Him in sincerity and express our anxiety and confusion. God wants us to be honest with Him—after all, He already knows what's in our hearts and minds.

While searching Scriptures, I found it quite interesting that many biblical saints struggled to understand certain things that happened in their lives. For example, Moses, Joshua, the psalmist David, the faithful man Job, and the loyal prophet Habakkuk asked why. Even Jesus Christ, God-Man incarnate who knew all things and never sinned, asked, "My God, my God, why hast thou forsaken me?" (Matthew 27:46). Ultimately, I believe these words were recorded for our benefit.

I have also struggled with certain issues that caused me to ask why. After several months of searching for answers, one cold December morning, I was prompted to get out of bed. After going to the kitchen table with a cup of coffee, I reached for my Bible. I opened my Bible to John 17:4 and began reading. Immediately I knew God was revealing His answer to me. Once I finished reading, He said to me, "Rest in these words: have peace."

My dear friend, I don't know your story. But perhaps you too have questioned God in light of a personal trial or tragedy. If anyone can empathize with you, it is God Himself. He understands your struggles and He wants you to come to Him when you have questions. Whether you get an answer or not, please remain faithful and trust Him with the elements of your life that are too complex for you to understand.

Your Reflections

He revealeth the deep and secret things: he knoweth what is in the darkness, and the light dwelleth (Daniel 2:22).

A New Direction

◆◆◆

I DON'T KNOW WHERE I AM AND HOW I GOT HERE. There are times in our lives when we have no idea where we are going or how we arrived at a certain location. Without distinct direction and especially in unfamiliar territory, our traveling experience can become difficult and somewhat frustrating.

However, today most of us are fortunate enough to own a GPS (Global Positioning System), which determines a precise location and provides a highly accurate speed and time. Ultimately, it makes it easier in getting to our destinations.

Oftentimes, we think we know the direction and details of our lives, and we head off without consulting God. We immediately start searching for shortcuts and bypasses, hoping that these can make life's journey a lot easier. Unfortunately, we end up at a dead end or an unfamiliar place overwhelmed with disappointment and frustration. Psalm 25:4 (NLT) echoes this truth. "Show me the path where I should walk, O LORD; point out the right road for me to follow."

When unfavorable things happen in our lives and we are forced to redirect our journey, we must trust and rely on our spiritual GPS (God's Positioning System). He is familiar with the territory and knows what lies ahead. His directions are very detailed, giving us mile markers and specific landmarks to guide us along the way. He instructs us when to be cautious, when to stop, or when to go. He even alerts us when to detour if there is construction ahead or if there has been an accident. God will safely lead us to our destination.

Our heavenly Father never intended for us to travel on our journey without his directions. He has simply instructed us to rely on Him while navigating through life's circumstances. If we follow His directions, we will never get off our path and lose our way. Trust Him today! His navigational skills are unfailing and much more dependable than our own self-direction.

Your Reflections

_____

_____

_____

_____

_____

_____

_____

_____

_____

_____

_____

_____

_____

_____

_____

_____

_____

_____

_____

_____

_____

_____

_____

_____

_____

_____

Trust in the LORD with all thine heart; and lean not unto thine own understanding (Proverbs 3:5).

The Power of Love

◆ ◆ ◆

AS I LANDED ON THE FRONT PORCH, it took all the courage that I had within me to make a stab at the doorbell. Finally, with one soft touch, I could hear the sound of the doorbell singing its familiar tune: *ding-dong.* In seconds, the door opened wide and the woman who stood behind the door looked very surprised, while gazing in the eyes of someone whom she had never seen. Although her countenance appeared to be very warm and pleasant, I could still detect her reservations on letting me enter. I introduced myself by name, stating that I had recently become a widow. "I am very harmless," I replied. She immediately invited me into her single-family home where her husband sat in his reclined chair. It was obvious that God's presence dwelled there.

On this particular day, I was overwhelmed with the burdens of life. I felt the loneliness and the emptiness of being a young widow. I felt like I had been forgotten and alienated from a world that I once knew. However, God proved His faithfulness once again when He placed me in the arms of this lovely elderly couple who took me in and loved me as their very own. I am grateful for the many meals that have been prepared by them and the warm hugs that constantly reminded me that I was loved. It was only God that allowed this woman to let a total stranger into her home, not knowing what to expect. Moreover, our relationship has bonded and they have embraced me with a love that I will never forget.

For many of us, it is easy to show love to our family and friends and to the people who we know. But it's another thing when a stranger shows up on our doorstep without warning. In Deuteronomy 10:19, the Israelites were instructed by God, "Love ye therefore the stranger: for ye were strangers in the Land of Egypt."

Our daily prayer should be that God will grant us the grace to love well. The power of His love is shown through us when we reach out to those in need. You will be surprised how a kind word, a hug, or a handshake can send a stranger a little farther on his journey.

Your Reflections

_____

_____

_____

_____

_____

_____

_____

_____

_____

_____

_____

_____

_____

_____

_____

_____

_____

_____

_____

_____

_____

_____

_____

_____

_____

_____

_____

Great are thy tender mercies, O LORD: quicken me according to thy judgments (Psalm 119:156).

Who Am I?

♦♦♦

"WHO ARE YOU?" I ASKED. Who is that person that is looking back at me from the mirror?" There I was, lying in bed around 5:00 a.m. Sunday morning, awakened from my sleep with a piercing feeling of dread. It felt like I had swallowed a sharp-edge rock and it had settled in the pit of my belly. With all the strength I could muster, I made a leap to the floor and looked into the long and shiny mirror that was mounted on the bathroom wall. Suddenly, I was startled by a strange image that reflected from the mirror. The reflection was an image of a woman who had lost her identity. She was accustomed to being called a wife, a helpmate, a sweetheart, a companion, and even beloved. I became overwhelmed and baffled as I stood and stared at the image. I didn't recognize *me*. "Oh God," I cried, "help me find myself; help me to know who I am."

Most often, we are defined by the roles we play in life, our accomplishments, and the way others perceive us. The things of this world are temporal, and when life takes an unexpected turn, it can lead to disappointment. However, when we take on the identity of Christ, He offers an eternal hope that gives us contentment and satisfaction.

I can boldly proclaim that my true identity lies in Christ and I am everything He says I am. He tells me, "I am the Lamb's wife and I will one day be in permanent union with Him." He calls me "the apple of His eye because I am His sweetheart and He loves me with an everlasting love." He took special interest in me by creating me a "helpmeet." Therefore, I am eager to help him wherever and whenever I am needed. He takes great pleasure in calling me His "companion." We laugh together, we commune together, and out of our relationship, He gives me great strength.

Furthermore, He makes me feel like a princess when He tells me that I am beautiful and I am His "beloved one," whom He will eternally cherish. After all, when I look in the mirror, my reflection is not *me*. It's a clear image of who I am in Christ.

Your Reflections

_____

_____

_____

_____

_____

_____

_____

_____

_____

_____

_____

_____

_____

_____

_____

_____

_____

_____

_____

_____

_____

_____

_____

_____

_____

Therefore if any man be in Christ, he is a new creature: old things are passed away; behold, all things are become new (2 Corinthians 5:17).

A Far-Away God

♦ ♦ ♦

DAVID WROTE, "WHY DO YOU STAND AFAR OFF, OH LORD? Why standest thou afar off, O LORD? why hidest thou thyself in times of trouble?" (Psalm 10:1). It is not always easy to react with a brave and courageous attitude while dealing with life's circumstances. However, the Old Testament gives us a biblical example of one man who struggled to remain positive while navigating through the desert times in his life. David, a spiritual giant, a man after God's own heart, was not afraid to spill his guts when he felt alone and abandoned by God. While we can all appreciate his honesty, his thoughts were not kept in the silence of his heart. He mustered up enough courage to ask, "God, where are you? Why do you seem to hide from me when I need you the most?"

Much like David, I have found myself in situations where I could not find traces of God. I longed to feel His presence, and I so desperately wanted Him to remind me that He was close by. Yet He remained at a distance and kept His silence. Although I felt shunned by Him, He was definitely at work. Once I turned my focus back to Him, I was able to recognize that the impressions of His handprints were on every situation, which was sure proof that He had been with me all along.

So often, we allow our circumstances to cloud our view of seeing God's hand. Ultimately, God wants us to trust Him and let the evidence reveal the truth. Proverbs 3:5 instructs us, "Trust in the Lord with all our heart; and lean not unto thine own understanding."

My friend, your experience may indicate that God is in the far distance. The truth is that God is not far from you at all. Even David later admits, "The LORD is nigh unto all them that call upon Him, to all that call upon Him in truth" (Psalm 145:18).

Let me encourage you with this thought: you can rejoice in the promise that God is always there and ready to listen. He is always ready to love you through each and every circumstance that life may thrust upon you.

Your Reflections

_____

_____

_____

_____

_____

_____

_____

_____

_____

_____

_____

_____

_____

_____

_____

_____

_____

_____

_____

_____

_____

_____

_____

_____

_____

_____

*But when they in their trouble did turn unto the Lord God of Israel,
and sought him, he was found of them (2 Chronicles 15:4).*

Play Your Hand Well

◆◆◆

IN A GAME OF POKER, YOU NEVER NOW WHAT KIND OF HAND you are going to be dealt. Sometimes, you may be dealt what appears to be a losing hand; however, the key is to make the best of what you have been given. So it is with life. One thing for certain is you can't predict what's going to happen day to day. You must prepare yourself to play the hand you are dealt.

When my late husband was diagnosed with cancer, my hand became difficult to play. I wanted to say, "I'm out," but I had to make the choice to get tough and rise up to the challenge. Although I didn't know what the final outcome would be, I knew I had to perform at my very best while maintaining a good perspective on life.

Card players may say they got lucky and won the game, but from a spiritual viewpoint, I understand that winning in the game of life is placing our total trust in God. We have to cling to what we know is true and learn His strategy of how to win when the odds are against us.

I don't know what your circumstances are. Maybe you have been dealt a job loss, the loss of a loved one, or betrayal by someone. You may be going through an ugly divorce or a terminal illness. Even if this is so, it doesn't mean you have a losing hand. It means you have to play your hand well.

Be encouraged knowing that you are a winner. Romans 8:37 tells us, "We are more than conquers through Him that loved us." So when good things happen, rejoice that God has given us more than we deserve, and if you happen to draw what appears to be a bad hand, rejoice that He has let you in on Christ's sufferings.

Your Reflections

_____

_____

_____

_____

_____

_____

_____

_____

_____

_____

_____

_____

_____

_____

_____

_____

_____

_____

_____

_____

_____

_____

_____

_____

These things I have spoken unto you, that in me ye might have peace.
In the world ye shall have tribulation: but be of good cheer; I have
overcome the world (John 16:33).

Lord, I Want to Be Whole

♦♦♦

WHEN WILL I GET MY LIFE BACK? Will I ever overcome the brokenness of life to be made whole again? Perhaps these were the weary thoughts that consumed the mind of this woman whose life was put on hold for twelve years.

The story of this woman unfolds in the accounts of Matthew, Mark, and Luke. We are told that she had a constant "issue of blood" upon her for twelve years. She may have become anemic while experiencing great weakness. This condition stole her peace and joy. According to the Leviticus law, she was considered unclean. Therefore, she was an outcast of society. She had no contact with her family and friends, and she was even barred from the place of worship. She suffered at the hands of many doctors while they tried to remedy her condition with countless medical treatments, but to no avail. With every appointment came disappointment. I can only imagine the pain her broken heart felt when she was finally told, "There is nothing more we can do." She spent everything she had trying to get well, but it seemed there was no hope.

> My dear friend, keep in mind that when men fail,
> Christ succeeds. "What is impossible with man
> is possible with God" (Luke 18:27). (NIV)

There is no way anyone can sugarcoat the anguish this woman experienced. She did not give up. Instead, she took a leap of faith by saying, "Enough is enough." Then she heard about Jesus, and suddenly her faith ignited. While running to meet Jesus, she pushed her way through the massive crowd that surrounded Him. She came up behind Him, reaching out in faith and touching the hem of His garment, and immediately the flow of blood stopped. It is revealed in Luke 8:48 that Jesus responded by saying, "Daughter, be of good comfort: thy faith has made thee whole; go in peace."

Can you relate to this woman with the "issue of blood?" Have you been dealing with certain issues that have lasted longer than you wanted? Have you been told that your case is hopeless? You may have been told it's too late; it's over. However, whatever issues you are dealing with, look to Jesus. Just a touch of Him can make you whole again.

Your Reflections

_____

_____

_____

_____

_____

_____

_____

_____

_____

_____

_____

_____

_____

_____

_____

_____

_____

_____

_____

_____

_____

_____

_____

_____

_____

_____

_____

_____

_____

Behold, I will bring it health and cure, and I will cure them, and will reveal unto them the abundance of peace and truth (Jeremiah 33:6).

Do Not Disturb

◆◆◆

"PEACE I LEAVE WITH YOU, my peace I give unto you: not as the world giveth, give I unto you. Let not your heart be troubled, neither let it be afraid" (John 14:27). These words reveal the intimacy that I have with my heavenly Father. They show His concern and His deep love that He has for me when I am faced with the fears and worries of this life.

No matter how hard we try to get away from them, we are not absent from the fears and worries of this world. Circumstances happen, situations arise, and we are left trying to handle them on our own, only to leave us exhausted and drained of our peace. But here's the good news: since peace is not dependent upon ourselves, it is absolute that we must depend upon the Prince of Peace who is our one and true source.

I know it is easier said than done, but don't waste another minute worrying about your problems. Give them to God, and let Him handle them. It may be a good idea to put a "Do Not Disturb" sign on the door of your heart, stopping all outside disturbances from gaining entry and stealing your peace. The Devil will take every opportunity to destroy your peace and tranquility. "The thief cometh not, but for to steal, and to kill, and to destroy: I am come that they might have life, and that they might have it more abundantly" (John 10:10).

Christ cares about you deeply. He knows about your unfulfilled desires, your broken dreams, your disappointments, and your defeats. He knows all the things that are troubling you. There is nothing that has transpired in your life that He is not aware of. So please take comfort in knowing that in the midst of these disturbing times, He longs for a close relationship with you so you may walk in His perfect peace.

Finally, I want to encourage you with these words that are recorded in John 16:33. "These things I have spoken unto you, that in me ye might have peace. In the world ye shall have tribulation: but be of good cheer; I have overcome the world."

Your Reflections

_____

_____

_____

_____

_____

_____

_____

_____

_____

_____

_____

_____

_____

_____

_____

_____

_____

_____

_____

_____

_____

_____

_____

_____

_____

_____

_____

_____

And the peace of God, which passeth all understanding, shall keep your hearts and minds through Christ Jesus (Philippians 4:7).

Showing Your True Colors

◆ ◆ ◆

THE OWNER OF A CERTAIN RESTAURANT GREETED me with a big hello and said, "You are always happy and you always have a big smile on your face." I was encouraged by his comment, so I responded with a courteous thank-you. However, his comment snagged my attention, causing me to pause for a brief moment to think about my childhood.

When I was growing up as a young girl, most people called me Smiley. However, smiling for me was part of my family trait, and in most cases, we could be identified as siblings just by our infectious smiles. Unlike my childhood, life experiences have definitely tested my smiley face. So do I put on a happy face and pretend like everything is okay? Let's not get it twisted. I may not always be happy with the things that transpire in my life, but now I certainly understand what it means to "count it all joy." It is my choice to have joy—and the joy that's in my heart shows on my face.

I don't think that Jesus was necessarily *happy* while suffering a cruel death, but I would imagine that He still had joy in spite of it all. The Bible explains it best in Hebrews 12:2. "Looking unto Jesus the author and finisher of our faith; who for the joy that was set before him endured the cross, despising the shame, and is set down at the right hand of the throne of God."

Don't give up, my friend. Don't allow your situation to be a joy buster. You may feel that no matter how hard you try, life's challenges seem to become more complicated. But during these times, James encourages you to *rejoice.* "When tests and challenges come at you from all sides. You know that under pressure your faith-life is forced into the open and shows its true colors" (James 1:2–4). (MSG)

No matter what your circumstances may look like in the natural, hold your chin high, put a big smile on your face, and let your joy shine through.

Your Reflections

_____

_____

_____

_____

_____

_____

_____

_____

_____

_____

_____

_____

_____

_____

_____

_____

_____

_____

_____

_____

_____

_____

_____

_____

_____

The LORD is my strength and my shield; my heart trusted in him, and I am helped: therefore my heart greatly rejoiceth; and with my song I will praise him (Psalm 28:7).

It Takes One to Know One

♦ ♦ ♦

ONLY A PERSON WITH IDENTICAL CHARACTER TRAITS would be able to recognize those traits in someone else. Perhaps it can be better said, "It takes one to know one." Certainly, this holds true for empathy in suffering as well. You can't understand the grief of a widow until you've suffered the loss of a spouse. You can't grasp the pain of a divorcee if you have not experienced the heartache of a divorce. It would be hard for you to identify with a barren woman if you have had the pleasure of bearing children. And you certainly wouldn't be able to empathize with the fear and dread of a terminal illness unless you or someone you love had been diagnosed with it.

But when you have suffered—I mean *really* suffered—you certainly have the credentials of being the one who can truly understand those who are experiencing certain trials. Moreover, your trials will equip you to become one of God's greatest conduits for those who are in distress, while sharing the comfort and consolation you received from time alone with Him.

We are told, "He comes alongside us when we go through hard times, and before you know it, He brings us alongside someone else who is going through hard times so that we can be there for that person just as God was there for us" (2 Corinthians 1:4). (MSG)

> Do you need encouraging today? Do you need someone to embrace you and compassionately say, "I understand, I've been there"? Jesus certainly understands the full scope of what you are going through, and He can get you through it. Trust in Him, because He has truly been there and done that!

My friend, encouragement is priceless to the one who is hurting. Therefore, we must seize every opportunity to help lift souls out of despair, thereby, helping them regain their footing in order for them to move a step farther.

Your Reflections

_____

_____

_____

_____

_____

_____

_____

_____

_____

_____

_____

_____

_____

_____

_____

_____

_____

_____

_____

_____

_____

_____

_____

_____

The LORD hath appeared of old unto me, saying, Yea, I have loved thee with an everlasting love: therefore with lovingkindness have I drawn thee (Jeremiah 31:3).

Life's Forecast

◆ ◆ ◆

I COULD TELL SOMETHING WAS DIFFERENT, but I couldn't figure out what it was. Finally, it dawned on me that a storm had hit the area earlier in the day and the huge oak tree that once dominated the view in my neighbor's front yard was no longer standing. The oak tree lay on the ground, uprooted from its clayed soil and its branches shattered to pieces. The oak tree looked strong and resilient and full of substance, but its roots were shallow; therefore, it was not strong enough to weather the storm.

We all are like trees subjected to the stormy elements of life. If our roots are shallow, we will either snap or uproot from our foundation. However, if our roots are nourished with the right nutrients, we will become grounded and grow stronger. Let's consider Jeremiah 17:8.

> For he shall be as a tree planted by the waters, and that spreadeth out her roots by the river, and shall not see when heat cometh, but her leaf shall be green; and shall not be careful in the year of drought, neither shall cease from yielding fruit.

Throughout our lives, we will encounter the storms of life. We may not be given a weather alert or a day-to-day forecast to let us know when they are coming, but we can prepare daily by grounding ourselves in God's Word. His Word, which is our support system, makes us stronger. Therefore, when we're surrounded by the black clouds, the heavy rain, and the raging wind, we will not be easily moved.

Proverbs 10:25 declares, "As the whirlwind passeth, so is the wicked no more: but the righteous is an everlasting foundation." Life's forecast may indicate a few storms coming your way, but the Son is still shining on the other side of those dark clouds, and He will eventually break through.

Your Reflections

_____

_____

_____

_____

_____

_____

_____

_____

_____

_____

_____

_____

_____

_____

_____

_____

_____

_____

_____

_____

_____

_____

_____

_____

_____

_____

_____

*And he shall be like a tree planted by the rivers of water, that bringeth
forth his fruit in his season; his leaf also shall not wither; and
whatsoever he doeth shall prosper (Psalm 1:3).*

First Responder

♦ ♦ ♦

AT SOME POINT IN OUR LIVES, WE ALL HAVE relied on EMTs, paramedics, dispatchers, firefighters, police officers, chaplains, and pastors. These people are called first responders, and I consider them some of the most courageous and dedicated people in the world. It doesn't matter what the weather is like, it doesn't matter what time of the day it is, and it doesn't even matter what they are involved in at the moment. They are always set on go, ready to jump into action whenever the tone sounds. They do this in regards to helping others, and as a result, many lives are saved. I often consider the fact that first responders wear a very heavy badge while they sacrifice, protect, and even lay their lives on the line.

John 15:13 reveals a great truth. "Greater love has no man than this, that a man lay down his life for his friends." Jesus certainly showed us the extent of His great love while being inflicted with physical trauma. He gave Himself up by suffering the most bitter and agonizing death in order for us to live. He bore our sins, our pain, our sicknesses, and every other trauma that we have ever encountered. Moreover, it is obvious that Jesus responded to the call. One of His greatest promises is found in

Psalm 50:15. (NASB) "Call upon me in the day of trouble; I will rescue you, and you will honor me."

> You may be suffering from an unbearable trauma
> that is in stable or maybe critical condition. Perhaps
> you are just hanging on by life support. Whatever
> your case may be, God is with you even in the most
> tragic call. He responds with great power, and He is
> willing and ready to deliver you from all destruction.

There is life beyond the lights and sirens. At the sound and flash of each emergency, there is hope, meaning you are still alive and help is on the way. Always remember God is your first responder.

Your Reflections

_____

_____

_____

_____

_____

_____

_____

_____

_____

_____

_____

_____

_____

_____

_____

_____

_____

_____

_____

_____

_____

_____

_____

_____

_____

_____

*In this was manifested the love of God toward us, because that God sent
his only begotten Son into the world, that we might live through him
(1 John 4:9).*

It Is Well

◆ ◆ ◆

I HAVE HAD THE OPPORTUNITY TO GET the inside story of a woman who was described as "great." She was known for her many acts of kindness, and her heart was built to serve God and His people. I can honestly say that this Shunammite woman was my kind of a woman. She was incredible, knowing very well that her son was dead, but she still replied, "It is well."

The story is told in the fourth chapter of 2 Kings when God makes a promise to this woman through His prophet Elisha. She was also generous, and she catered to the needs of the prophet. Her hospitality was rewarded by the gift of a son.

Elisha said, "About this season, according to the time of life, thou shalt embrace a son" (2 Kings 4:16). At first, she couldn't believe it. She did not want to be misled and become swallowed up in the disappointment of an empty promise. Ultimately, the promise took form just as Elisha had said it would. Moreover, the boy grew older but later became ill and died.

As we look further, we find that the tenacity of this great woman was extraordinary. She took the dead boy inside and placed him on the bed. Then she went and found the prophet.

When she found him, she basically said, "I didn't ask for this! This was all your idea, so fix it!"

Let's consider the outcome. Her son was restored to life because of her faith and her positive confession. Sometimes, we are afraid to dream and hope because of what we may to face later. But as we observe the devotion of the Shunammite woman, we realize she was not about to let go of her son without a fight. So you too refuse to let go of what God has already promised you.

You may not have the ability to revive the dead dreams and promises, but you do have the ability to trust God to fix it. No matter how bad your situation may seem, keep confessing and reminding yourself, "It is well."

Proverbs 10:22 teaches us, "The blessing of the LORD, it maketh rich, and he addeth no sorrow with it."

Your Reflections

_____

_____

_____

_____

_____

_____

_____

_____

_____

_____

_____

_____

_____

_____

_____

_____

_____

_____

_____

_____

_____

_____

_____

_____

Now he that ministereth seed to the sower both minister bread for your food, and multiply your seed sown, and increase the fruits of your righteousness (2 Corinthians 9:10).

Will Your Anchor Hold?

♦ ♦ ♦

"I'LL HUFF AND I'LL PUFF AND I'LL BLOW YOUR HOUSE DOWN!" You have probably heard this classic line at least once in your lifetime, which was spoken by the big, bad wolf in the fairy tale "The Three Little Pigs." However, I am fascinated by the fact that there is much truth in the moral of the story: making good decisions pays off in the long haul.

Moreover, let us consider the parable that Jesus gave in Matthew 7:24–27. (NIV)

> Therefore everyone who hears these words of mine and puts them into practice is like a wise man who built his house on the rock. The rain came down, the streams rose, and the winds blew and beat against that house; yet it did not fall, because it had its foundation on the rock. But everyone who hears these words of mine and does not put them into practice is like a foolish man who built his house on sand. The rain came down, the streams rose, and the winds blew and beat against that house, and it fell with a great crash.

This parable gives every indication that before the storms came, these two houses looked identical. They may have both been beautiful, spacious, and comfortable. On the surface, you couldn't really tell which house was built on the sand and which was anchored deep to the rock. It was only when the storms hit that you could see the difference in the homes. So it is with us. It's impossible to tell who we really are when things are going well. But the stormy seasons reveal the strength of our foundation.

> Is your footing dug deep enough? Will your
> anchor hold when the storms of life come your
> way? Nevertheless, if you have invested time
> in laying a biblical foundation, you will not be
> disappointed. It will pay off in the long haul.

My dear friend, please be assured that destruction is the very nature of Satan. His ultimate goal is to kill, steal, and destroy. No matter how hard he huffs and puffs and tries to blow your house down, he can never destroy that which is built on the solid rock. The next time he shows up at your house, tell him to go away because he's wasting his breath.

Your Reflections

_____

_____

_____

_____

_____

_____

_____

_____

_____

_____

_____

_____

_____

_____

_____

_____

_____

_____

_____

_____

_____

_____

Nevertheless the foundation of God standeth sure, having this seal, The Lord knoweth them that are his. And, let every one that nameth the name of Christ depart from iniquity (2 Timothy 2:19).

Beauty for Ashes

◆ ◆ ◆

THIS WOMAN MUST HAVE BEEN ON THE DOWNSIDE of life after going through several failed marriages. She must have felt twice an outcast and perhaps was rated number one as being despised and rejected in her own town. Her struggle with shame, depression, and low self-esteem may have been a constant reminder that her life was in shambles, and everyone in the village knew it. Having endured such emotional stress, she taught herself how to deaden the pain.

Avoiding the other women in the village, she chose to draw water in the parching heat of the day. The other women of Samaria gathered water in the cool of the morning, using this opportunity to visit and talk. Instead of embracing her, there is a good chance they made her the highlight of their conversation. I can only imagine how the hurtful gossip traveled throughout the entire village of Samaria. This woman, whose life was no more than a heap of ashes, one day met Jesus at the well, and He uniquely transformed her life into something extraordinarily beautiful.

Maybe you are in a firestorm and the flames of
fire are dancing all around you. Perhaps the heat
is more than you can bear. You may wonder, *How*

long will I wake up to the dreadful mornings only to face disappointment? You may even struggle with the fact that your life is too messed up for God to fix. However, take joy in knowing that when the blaze dies down and nothing is left but the cold black ashes, God will give you beauty in exchange for your ashes. Isaiah 61:3 (NKJV) tells us, "He came to console those who mourn in Zion, To give them beauty for ashes, The oil of joy for mourning, The garment of praise for the spirit of heaviness; That they may be called trees of righteousness, The planting of the Lord, that He may be glorified."

It doesn't matter who you are or what you have done; Jesus loves you despite all the shameful and wretched things that have happened in your life. He takes pleasure in whatever you give Him that is tangled and messed up. "Therefore if any man be in Christ, he is a new creature: old things are passed away; behold, all things are become new" (2 Corinthians 5:17).

Your Reflections

_____

_____

_____

_____

_____

_____

_____

_____

_____

_____

_____

_____

_____

_____

_____

_____

_____

_____

_____

_____

_____

_____

_____

_____

_____

_____

_____

_____

*He that believeth on me, as the Scripture hath said, out of his belly
shall flow rivers of living water (John 7:38).*

The Attitude of Mary

♦ ♦ ♦

ONE INSTRUCTOR ASKED his audience, "How many of you woke up this morning with an attitude?" Needless to say, no one in the room raised their hand. Unfortunately, our minds have been programmed to think negative, when we think in terms of attitude. My theory is that when we arise each morning, we all have an attitude, whether it is a good one or a bad one. Ultimately, we tend to allow our experiences to determine what type of attitude we possess for that day.

In the New Testament's account of John, we are told that Mary, the sister of Martha and Lazarus, had such love for Jesus that she placed her whole focus at His feet while listening to His words. Mary loved Jesus so greatly that she anointed His feet with a costly bottle of perfume while wiping His feet with her hair. But when her brother Lazarus became ill, then died, her attitude changed. Like Mary, it's easy to develop a negative attitude when circumstances hit hard. But it's a matter of keeping the right focus while choosing to find the good.

Yes, it may be true that you have faced
some challenging times. The question
is this: how did you react?

The wrong attitude will most likely bring on wrong results. Therefore, we must keep our attitude in check, and it should always reflect the attitude of Christ. In Philippians 2:5, Paul exhorts us to "Let this mind be in you, which was also in Christ Jesus." Jesus is our ultimate example of how we are to behave and conduct ourselves when we encounter these challenging times. Let's choose each day to keep a good attitude regardless of what each day may bring. Hang in there. Your troubles will never defeat you, as long as you keep the right attitude.

Your Reflections

_____

_____

_____

_____

_____

_____

_____

_____

_____

_____

_____

_____

_____

_____

_____

_____

_____

_____

_____

_____

_____

_____

_____

*My brethren, count it all joy when ye fall into divers temptations
(James 1:2).*

Navigating through Life's Obstacles

♦♦♦

HAVE YOU EVER BEEN DRIVING ALONG THE ROADWAY, enjoying a smooth ride, when all of a sudden you were caught off guard by hitting a roadblock in the road? If so, perhaps this roadblock detoured you from your original plan. While no one can escape life's obstacles, remember that God can take your difficult experience and develop something much greater than you can ever imagine.

I was blessed after receiving an encouraging card from a very special person. The outside of the card displayed a beautiful scene of the flowing waters of a springtime stream, with a message that read, "Our character is revealed while navigating life's obstacles." What a powerful message! It's amazing that our characters can never be developed in the good and quiet times of life. Only through the stream of trials and tribulations is the authentic person revealed.

Granted, I have had my share of obstacles. But in each circumstance, I trusted in God's ability to bring me out victoriously. Although the obstacles seemed to be working against me, they were actually working for me.

Romans 8:28 declares, "And we know that all things work together for good to them that love God, to them who are the called according to his purpose."

> If you are faced with obstacles in your pathway, my
> dear friend, I want to encourage you to not become
> weary. Keep trusting God, for He is working
> something out far greater than what actually
> appears. His love will sustain you, and He will
> remain with you no matter how hard it may get.

The path of your victory has been set, and the Enemy cannot destroy it as long as you keep your faith in Christ.

Your Reflections

_____

_____

_____

_____

_____

_____

_____

_____

_____

_____

_____

_____

_____

_____

_____

_____

_____

_____

_____

_____

_____

_____

Teach me thy way, O LORD, and lead me in a plain path, because of mine enemies (Psalm 27:11).

Mirror, Mirror on the Wall

♦ ♦ ♦

AS I WAS GETTING READY TO START MY DAY, I couldn't help but laugh at my own image reflecting in the mirror. My hair looked like it had been in a furious windstorm, with each strand standing in several directions. My facial appearance looked as though I had been in a boxing match and lost. I thought, *Girl, you look a hot mess.* I looked so bad that for a split second, I thought my mirror was distorted. However, that was certainly not the case. The mirror truly revealed the reflection of what I really looked like, and my reflection reminded me that I was in need of improvement before going out to meet the world. In fact, there was nothing presentable about my appearance. There was work to be done.

Our spiritual walk is somewhat the same. The mirror of God's Word shows us who we really are and what we can become. When we look in the mirror, we can walk away and forget about what we saw or we can make the necessary changes in order to become presentable to God and others.

The apostle James tells us,

> But be ye doers of the word, and not hearers only, deceiving your own selves. For if any be a hearer of the

word, and not a doer, he is like unto a man beholding his natural face in a glass: For he beholdeth himself, and goeth his way, and straightway forgetteth what manner of man he was. But whoso looketh into the perfect law of liberty, and continueth therein, he being not a forgetful hearer, but a doer of the work, this man shall be blessed in his deed (James 1:22-25).

When the world sees you, do you look a hot mess? Do they see the reflection of Christ by the love and compassion that you show to others? Too often, His reflection in us is distorted by our wrongful attitudes, unforgiveness, and even our harmful speech.

Remember His mirror does not reflect false images. It reflects truth, it keeps us in check, and it shows us what we need to fix or change. It may be worth asking, "Mirror, mirror on the wall, am I a reflection of Christ at all?"

Your Reflections

So God created man in his own image, in the image of God he created him; male and female he created them (Genesis 1:27).

The Bitter Cup

♦♦♦

ONE LADY STATED, "I AM FACED WITH MAKING A DIFFICULT DECISION." As she began to share her story, my thoughts reflected back to the story of Jesus when He was in the garden of Gethsemane. Jesus was facing one of the most difficult times of his life. He was greatly distressed and troubled. The weight of the world was upon Him because of our sins and His coming suffering. He looked upon Himself a brutal death that even caused Him to sweat big drops of blood. I can only imagine my Savior's indescribable pain as He suffered the bitter agony of being alone, abandoned, and betrayed. He was at a crossroad, having to make a decision that would affect the whole world. Just hours away from facing the rugged cross, He fell with His face to the ground and prayed. "O my Father, if it be possible, let this cup pass from me: nevertheless not as I will, but as thou wilt" (Matthew 26:39).

> Are you experiencing a bitter cup? You may be in
> the midst of a season of loneliness, abandonment, or
> rejection. No matter how bitter your cup may be,
> don't give up. God loves you, and He cares for you.

Just as Jesus knew His suffering was for a purpose, you too must realize that God has designed you for a unique and special purpose. His will for your life is perfect, and you can be assured that He will be with you every step of the way. "And the LORD, he it is that doth go before thee; he will be with thee, he will not fail thee, neither forsake thee: fear not, neither be dismayed" (Deuteronomy 31:8).

Your Reflections

_____

_____

_____

_____

_____

_____

_____

_____

_____

_____

_____

_____

_____

_____

_____

_____

_____

_____

_____

_____

_____

_____

_____

_____

_____

_____

_____

_____

Trust in the Lord with all thine heart; and lean not unto thine own understanding. In all thy ways acknowledge him, and he shall direct thy paths (Proverbs 3:5-6).

It's Never Too Late

◆ ◆ ◆

I OFTEN REFLECT ON THOSE DARK AND DREARY DAYS walking down the long hallways of the hospital. Changing from one elevator to another, I would hurriedly run to my five-year-old son's bedside while he was being treated for acute nephritis (kidney disease). During the course of his illness, his body began to swell, along with developing high blood pressure. The side effect of the medication to treat the high blood pressure caused hair to cover his entire body.

We were disappointed when we were told by the urologist that medical reports were not in our favor, and doctors did not have the cure to make our son well. I could not fully process what was going on at that point. So I popped the big question. "What have I done to deserve this?" Psalm 34:19 declares, "Many are the afflictions of the righteous: but the Lord delivereth him out of them all."

At this point, the best information that the doctor could offer was to place our son back in school. However, we were faced with another dilemma of him being teased by other children concerning the facial hair.

Several months after our son was released from the hospital, God began to turn his health around. Over a two-year period, he was completely healed from this disease. I truly praise God for what He did, because He intervened on our behalf.

Are you facing a circumstance that seems impossible? Have you been told that there is no hope? I want to encourage you to trust in the Lord always. No matter how challenging your circumstances may be, or what the end results look like, it's never too late to trust God. "And he said, the things which are impossible with men are possible with God" (Luke 18:27).

Trust God with your impossibilities.

Your Reflections

_____

_____

_____

_____

_____

_____

_____

_____

_____

_____

_____

_____

_____

_____

_____

_____

_____

_____

_____

_____

_____

_____

_____

_____

_____

_____

_____

_____

"In God I will praise his word, in God I have put my trust; I will not fear what flesh can do unto me" (Psalm 56:4).

Love Is a Many Splendored Thing

♦ ♦ ♦

I DIDN'T BOTHER TO ASK, "Are you all right?" It was quite obvious that she wasn't.

At a Wal-Mart store, I observed a young lady who stood outside her vehicle with the hood lifted. Two small children occupied the back seat of the car while a gentleman, who I assumed was her husband, appeared to be searching for tools. The young lady stood with her head bowed with a stream of tears flowing down her cheeks. I could tell that she was not in the mood for talking, so I embraced her with a big hug. Hugging her as tightly as I could, I whispered, "It's going to be okay." She looked up at me, not knowing who I was, but still nodded her head yes.

As I proceeded toward the store, my eyes welled up with tears while being reminded of Romans 12:10–11. "Be kindly affectioned one to another with brotherly love; in honour preferring one another; Not slothful in business; fervent in spirit; serving the Lord;"

In many cases, we become the reflective mirror for God in revealing His true love to others. And sometimes, it is revealed through a hug or a kind word that can make them feel incredibly safe and secure.

With all that being said, I will admit I know what it's like to experience an abundance of God's love. It was His love that kept the fabric of my being woven together when I was falling apart. His love gave me strength to remain strong when I wanted to give up. His love was mirrored through my family and friends and those special people that He allowed to show up out of nowhere. However, God's love did not fail me, because His love is never ending. Jeremiah 31:3 says, "I have loved you with an everlasting love: therefore with loving kindness have I drawn thee."

My dear friend, if we desire to see more people drawn to Christ, then our prayer should be this: "Dear Lord, use us as vessels for sharing your love to the world and to those that are around us." It's true what the songwriter said. "Love is a many splendored thing." And it can be demonstrated to others in many different ways.

Your Reflections

_____

_____

_____

_____

_____

_____

_____

_____

_____

_____

_____

_____

_____

_____

_____

_____

_____

_____

_____

_____

_____

_____

_____

_____

By this shall all men know that ye are my disciples, if ye have love one to another (John 13:35).

The Roller-Coaster Ride

◆◆◆

FROM A DISTANCE, IT LOOKED LIKE A FUN RIDE. People were laughing, screaming, and throwing their hands in the air. Out of excitement, you decided to join in on all the fun. So you jumped onto the roller coaster, and at takeoff, the coaster began moving slowly. Then unexpectedly, you were lifted high in the air, only to dive back down at a high rate of speed. The short dips and the 180-degree turns caused your stomach to churn, but you braced yourself for the next move. Just when you thought the ride was over, the coaster suddenly took off again and started doing upside-down loops. Again, it accelerated then it slowed down again, and the next turn took you through a dark tunnel.

Sometimes, our lives can be parallel to a roller coaster. In 1 Kings 18 and 19, the Prophet Elijah shows an example of what it is like to be on a spiritual roller coaster. He, however, demonstrates great courage in the king's palace. He witnessed God's supply by the brook while being part of a great miracle that took place in the widow's home. He also witnessed the fire from heaven and the coming of the rain, but when his ride started going downhill, Elijah fled to a juniper tree. And from there, he prayed, "Lord, I have had enough! Take my life" (1 Kings 19:4). (NIV) The mighty prophet of God is discouraged and depressed, but God extends His mercy to him by sending an angel. "All at once the angel touched him and said, "Get up and eat" (1 Kings 19:5). (NIV)

> My dear friend, you don't have to tell me. I know
> that your ride has been rough lately. You may
> have hit the bottom of the drop. You may be going
> through the loop that turned your world upside
> down. But do not panic, and do not be afraid, for
> this ride will soon be over. This ride cannot be
> compared to the things that God has in store for you.

Please consider there are some things in life that are just part of the ride. So no matter how bumpy and uncomfortable it gets, keep holding on. And when the ride is over you will find that God was with you all along.

Your Reflections

Fear thou not; for I am with thee: be not dismayed; for I am thy God: I will strengthen thee; yea, I will help thee; yea, I will uphold thee with the right hand of my righteousness (Isaiah 41:10).

You've Messed with the Wrong One, Baby

♦ ♦ ♦

"BUT AS FOR YOU, YE THOUGHT EVIL AGAINST ME; but God meant it unto good" (Genesis 50:20). These are the words of Joseph, who was thrown in the pit by his brothers, and from the pit, he went straight to being a slave. He was later imprisoned for a crime he didn't commit. And for years, he suffered untold misery at the hands of cruel and unjust people, yet his heart remained pure. I would like to say that Joseph was not a man to be messed with. Though he endured much, God had his back, and God blessed him in everything he did. When the process was finished, God rewarded him by making him prime minister over all the land of Egypt. He became ruler over his own enemy.

You may realize that Joseph's life was not unusual. You too have dealt with your own pits of life. However, Psalm 40:1-2 says,

> I waited patiently for the LORD; and he inclined unto me, and heard my cry. He brought me up also out of an horrible pit, out of the miry clay, and set my feet upon a rock, and established my goings.

Joseph's life is so encouraging to me, and I hope it is encouraging to you as well. His life of testimonies confirms that it doesn't matter how deep we are in the pit. If we keep trusting in our Lord and Savior, He will keep us in perfect peace, giving us the strength to triumph over all.

As a child of God, He has given you the power to reign over your Enemy while preparing you for an expected end. What the Enemy meant for evil in your life God will turn around for your good.

> My dear friend, you are strong, you are courageous.
> You are God's mighty warrior. So when the
> Enemy comes again to cast you in the pit, tell him,
> "You've messed with the wrong one, baby."

Your Reflections

_____

_____

_____

_____

_____

_____

_____

_____

_____

_____

_____

_____

_____

_____

_____

_____

_____

_____

_____

_____

_____

_____

_____

_____

_____

He brought me up also out of an horrible pit, out of the miry clay, and set my feet upon a rock, and established my goings (Psalm 40:2).

He Saw the Best in You!

◆ ◆ ◆

WHAT DO YOU SEE WHEN YOU LOOK IN THE MIRROR? Do you see failure and disappointment, or do you see success and satisfaction? Many Christians tend to struggle with who they are and the way others may view them. However, we are not defined by the world's perspective; we are defined by who God says we are, and we must start seeing ourselves through His eyes. His spiritual eyes reveal the best in us.

Picture David when he was a young shepherd boy. Many knew him as the son of Jesse, just an ordinary, ruddy-faced handsome boy. But God saw a brave and courageous young man who later became Israel's greatest king. What about Moses? He was an eighty-year-old man, verbally impaired, who had already passed the average life span for his generation. Most would ask, "Is he the right man for the job? Isn't he too old to accomplish anything?" However, God saw a mild and meek leader who became the deliverer of His people. Gideon saw himself as the least in the tribe of Manasseh, but God saw a mighty man of valor. Jeremiah looked at himself as young and slow in speech, but God saw a great prophet for the nations.

Have you ever considered that God isn't looking for impressive people? Ultimately, He's looking for someone like you. So I admonish you to look up, look forward. Start viewing yourself as God sees you. He has fashioned you in His very own image, and when He created you and knitted you together inside your mother's womb, He saw the best in you!

Your Reflections

_____

_____

_____

_____

_____

_____

_____

_____

_____

_____

_____

_____

_____

_____

_____

_____

_____

_____

_____

_____

_____

_____

_____

_____

_____

Before I formed thee in the belly I knew thee; and before thou camest forth out of the womb I sanctified thee, and I ordained thee a prophet unto the nations (Jeremiah 1:5).

No Time to Go AWOL

◆ ◆ ◆

YOUNG TIMOTHY WAS AT HIS WIT'S END. His troubles seemed to multiply by the days. He seemed to face a spiritual battle, one after another. Perhaps, he was at the breaking point, ready to hang up his armor. It was in the midst of these challenges that the apostle Paul wrote Timothy and said. "Thou therefore endure hardness, as a good soldier of Jesus Christ" (2 Timothy 2:3).

Have you ever been in such an intense situation that you thought your mind might break? Or have you ever felt like you might collapse mentally from being pushed hard up against the wall, with no obvious way of escape? If the answer is yes, you may relate to what Timothy was going through at the time Paul wrote him. So what do you do? Do you keep fighting like Timothy, or do you go AWOL?

As I pen this devotional, I realize some of you are right in the middle of a heated battle. You may be contemplating going AWOL, but please be reminded that there is a big price to pay. I admonish you to stand strong and fight like a good soldier. Let's take another look at the letter Paul wrote to Timothy.

This charge I commit unto thee, son Timothy, according
to the prophecies which went before on thee, that thou
by them mightest war a good warfare; Holding faith,
and a good conscience; which some having put away
concerning faith have made shipwreck.
1 Timothy 1:18-19

Though the missiles of life may come to discourage you, they
will never defeat you as long as you walk in Christ. When you
follow Him and obey His commands, you and He together make
an invincible team that will utterly destroy the Enemy. And yes,
things may get worse before getting better, but keep in mind that
your commanding officer is an awesome God, and He has never
lost a battle.

Your Reflections

_____

_____

_____

_____

_____

_____

_____

_____

_____

_____

_____

_____

_____

_____

_____

_____

_____

_____

_____

_____

_____

_____

_____

_____

_____

_____

_____

_____

_____

But thy servants will pass over, every man armed for war, before the Lord to battle, as my lord saith (Numbers 32:27).

Obedience Is Better than Sacrifice

◆◆◆

QUEEN VASHTI AND KING AHASUERUS WERE THE ROYAL couple. The king made a feast which lasted for seven days (Esther 1:5). We are told that Queen Vashti made a feast for the women who had attended this special occasion with their husbands (Esther 1:9). In the midst of having a good time, things suddenly took a different turn when the king decided he wanted his wife, Queen Vashti, to appear at his feast to show off her beauty to all the men. When she refused the command to come, the king became angry and dethroned her from her position. Perhaps this was not a happy ending for Queen Vashti, and I am pretty sure that she never expected that her disobedience to the king would result in her being kicked to the curb.

This story somewhat challenges me to take a look at my own level of obedience. What part does my obedience play in God's plan for my life? How often have I missed out on His blessings because I made the decision to disobey Him? My obedience is merely doing what He asks of me, and trusting Him with the outcome.

What about you? Where does your level
of obedience fall on the scale?

Ultimately, we must allow God to be God, no matter what He asks of us. Whether it seems humiliating and embarrassing, we are obligated to obey Him. After all, He is our king.

"For this is the love of God, that we keep his commandments: and his commandments are not grievous" (1 John 5:3).

Your Reflections

_____

_____

_____

_____

_____

_____

_____

_____

_____

_____

_____

_____

_____

_____

_____

_____

_____

_____

_____

_____

_____

_____

_____

*Thou shalt keep therefore his statutes, and his commandments, which
I command thee this day, that it may go well with thee, and with thy
children after thee, and that thou mayest prolong thy days upon the
earth, which the L*ORD* thy God giveth thee, for ever
(Deuteronomy 4:40).*

Seasons of Life

◆ ◆ ◆

"AND HE SHALL BE LIKE A TREE planted by the rivers of water, that bringeth forth his fruit in his season; his leaf also shall not wither; and whatsoever he doeth shall prosper" (Psalm 1:3). Spring, summer, fall, and winter are seasons that we experience throughout the year. As each season transitions from one to the other, each will bring about a different meaning and purpose. When the spring season rolls around, we can see the rebirth and growth of the herbs and trees, while the summer months bring forth fruition and fulfillment. The fall season is a time for harvesting; the winter months slip in with the bitter coldness and barrenness. When we focus on each season, we are able to see the beauty of God's creation as well as appreciate his divine order and purpose.

Our lives are much the same as the seasons of nature. We go through seasonal changes, and with each change comes transition. The apostle Paul speaks to us about stripping away the old nature of man and taking on the new. If we are expecting elevation in Christ, a change must come.

You may be experiencing a season of rest, perhaps a season of barrenness, or maybe the time has come for you to harvest.

Whatever season you are in, be encouraged to know that God is with you. When the dry season comes, he will allow you to draw from the living waters and your roots will run deep and grow strong. In the dead of winter, He will renew your spirit and bring life back to your soul. He will not allow you to grow weary while you are laboring, for He will give you the strength to endure.

Be reminded of His incredible promise recorded in Psalm 128:2. (NIV) "You will eat the fruit of your labor; blessings and prosperity will be yours."

As you transition into the next season of your life, prepare yourself for the best and receive all that He has for you. May His everlasting love and peace be with you forevermore.

Your Reflections

_____

_____

_____

_____

_____

_____

_____

_____

_____

_____

_____

_____

_____

_____

_____

_____

_____

_____

_____

_____

_____

_____

_____

_____

_____

_____

To every thing there is a season, and a time to every purpose under the heaven (Ecclesiastes 3:1).

If Not for Grace

♦ ♦ ♦

CAN YOUR FAITH HOLD UP UNDER EXTREME PRESSURE? Is your faith strong enough to endure the malicious attacks of the Enemy? There are times when we are just plain worn out from dealing with Satan's attacks, and then we pray and hope that they will eventually go away.

We can find this example in the life of the apostle Paul. He was a great man of God, and God used him in a great way, but his life was anything but easy. As tough as it was, Paul's pain became too much to bear. We are told that He was given a thorn in the flesh, and though it is unknown to us, it was significant enough for him to ask God to take it away. His thorn was irritating and annoying, and after pleading with God three times to remove it, God replied, "My Grace is sufficient for thee" (2 Corinthians 12:9).

I believe that we all have a thorn in some way that we are dealing with. And keep in mind that just because we are children of God, it doesn't mean we are exempted from Satan's attacks. Moreover, he finds us as a perfect target.

> You may wonder, *How can I live with this thorn*
> *day in and day out?* You may feel that your

thorn is holding you back and has kept you from excelling. Don't be discouraged. "Be strong in the grace that is in Christ Jesus" (2 Timothy 2:1).

Satan may have put the thorn there to destroy you, but God can use it to define you. Satan may have put it there to curse you, but God can use it to bless you. Yes, my dear friend, God's grace is truly sufficient. His grace will get you through.

Your Reflections

_____

_____

_____

_____

_____

_____

_____

_____

_____

_____

_____

_____

_____

_____

_____

_____

_____

_____

_____

_____

_____

_____

_____

_____

_____

_____

*There hath no temptation taken you but such as is common to man:
but God is faithful, who will not suffer you to be tempted above that ye
are able; but will with the temptation also make a way to escape, that ye
may be able to bear it (1 Corinthians 10:13).*

Life in Reverse

♦ ♦ ♦

I RECALL HAVING A DREAM SOME TIME AGO that captured my attention. In the dream, I returned to my home only to find that it had been invaded. I could hear voices shouting from the inside of the home, so I realized the intruders were still on the premises. As I reached for my cell phone to call 911, a blue light appeared, letting me know that my phone had been blocked from all outgoing and incoming calls. I hurriedly returned to my vehicle to leave, and as I was backing out of the garage, the intruders began approaching me. My vehicle would not operate in drive; therefore, I had to drive the vehicle in reverse in order to get away. The invaders were after me so fast and furious that I thought at any moment they would capture me. As they continued chasing me, my vehicle eventually ran into a ditch, making a complete turnaround, and at this point, I was able to escape.

This is the message that I received from the dream: God can turn around any situation that seems hopeless.

Let's take a look at 1 Corinthians 10:13. (MSG) "No test or temptation that comes your way is beyond the course of what others have had to face." All you need to remember is that God

101

will never let you down. He'll never let you be pushed past your limit. He'll always be there to help you come through it.

This is a proven fact in the life of Joseph. Joseph went from the pit to Potiphar's house, from Potiphar's house to prison, and from prison to the palace. However, God was with him, and in the end, Joseph's situation was turned around.

Is there something happening in
your life that you need God to turn around? God
is faithful, and you can trust Him completely.
No matter how hopeless your circumstance may
appear, you can count on Him being there for you.
So when everything in your life seems to be going
in reverse, God can show up and turn it around.

Your Reflections

_____
_____
_____
_____
_____
_____
_____
_____
_____
_____
_____
_____
_____
_____
_____
_____
_____
_____
_____
_____
_____
_____
_____
_____
_____

The righteousness of the upright shall deliver them: but transgressors shall be taken in their own naughtiness (Proverbs 11:6).

Progressive Overload

◆ ◆ ◆

I COULD HARDLY WAIT TO RETURN TO THE LOCKER ROOM. I had reached the point of progressive overload and every muscle in my body was in pain. I thought, *I am not going to make it. I will be dead before Christmas.* He kept reminding me, "I do this every day, and I know how much you can take." Nevertheless, I continued to press through, and at the end of each set of repetitions, I would hear him say, "Good job!"

As a fitness professional, my son-in-law takes pride in training himself and others toward living a more productive and healthy lifestyle. However, it takes hard work and perseverance, and yes, the pain can be so severe at times that you will want to give up and quit. Ultimately, your goal is to press on, in order to receive the desired outcome. As it is often said, the human body will not change unless you force it to.

No one welcomes pain in their lives. We are never prepared for it; it's never convenient, and many times, it seems so unfair. Hebrews 12:11 (NIV) declares, "No discipline seems pleasant at the time, but painful. Later on, however, it produces a harvest of righteousness and peace for those who have been trained by it."

I never thought I would have made it this far after the passing of my beloved. There were times I literally thought I was going to lose my sanity and die from the overload on my mind, soul, and body. Ultimately, I find comfort knowing that my spiritual trainer is carefully watching over me and understands the depth of my pain. He knows exactly how much I am capable of bearing.

I've come to realize my faith is not as healthy as I thought. My spiritual workout needed improving, and now my faith is being pushed beyond its normal demand. But through my pain, I am learning how to become bigger and stronger, knowing that my pain shall bring me victory.

Perhaps you've been there too. Remember the overload principle is not meant to harm you; it is meant to improve your fitness. Your overload will allow you to create a faith that is more capable and fit than it was before.

Your Reflections

_____

_____

_____

_____

_____

_____

_____

_____

_____

_____

_____

_____

_____

_____

_____

_____

_____

_____

_____

_____

_____

_____

_____

For bodily exercise profiteth little: but godliness is profitable unto all things, having promise of the life that now is, and of that which is to come (1 Timothy 4:8).

The Heavyweight Champion

◆◆◆

MUHAMMAD ALI, WHO WAS THEN CASSIUS CLAY, was considered the greatest boxer of all time. He defeated reigning champion Sonny Liston for the world heavyweight title in 1964. The relentless Cassius Clay taunted Liston before the fight, promising to "float like a butterfly, sting like a bee." As well as predicting a knockout. When Liston failed to answer the bell at the start of the seventh round, Clay was indeed crowned heavyweight champion of the world. In the ring after the fight, the new champ roared, "I am the greatest!"

I pay tribute to this great boxer who accomplished so much during his boxing career, but I pay the greatest tribute to our Lord Jesus Christ. He never entered a boxing ring, He never appeared on the front cover of *Sports Illustrated*, nor did He hold a great name in any media. Yet there are countless books, songs, and poems that exalt His greatness throughout the world.

Furthermore, His greatness was demonstrated while suffering excruciating pain as those rusty nails held His body to wooden posts. In that moment, He took on the weight of sin of all mankind in the entire universe, becoming the heavyweight champion of the world. It is declared in 1 Peter 2:24 that, "Who his own self bare our sins in his own body on the tree,that we, being dead to sins, should live unto righteousness." He is, altogether, the greatest!

In closing, I want to remind you that Satan lost his title. He was knocked out and defeated over two thousand years ago. He no longer reigns over you; therefore, you can experience victory in all aspects of your life.

My dear friend, when your heart is overwhelmed and weighed down with the burdens of life, let the heavyweight champion of the world carry your load. His words of comfort are recorded in Matthew 11:28–30. (NIV)

> Come to me all of you who are weary and burdened, and I will give you rest. Take my yoke upon you and learn from me for I am gentle and humble in heart, and you will find rest for your souls. For my yoke is easy and my burden is light.

Your Reflections

_____

_____

_____

_____

_____

_____

_____

_____

_____

_____

_____

_____

_____

_____

_____

_____

_____

_____

_____

_____

_____

_____

_____

Looking unto Jesus the author and finisher of our faith; who for the joy that was set before him endured the cross, despising the shame, and is set down at the right hand of the throne of God (Hebrews 12:2).

Take Your Best Shot

♦ ♦ ♦

FROM CHILDHOOD, I KNEW I LOVED BASKETBALL, but I never dreamed of becoming a great player. It all began when my high school basketball coach recognized the potential that was hidden inside of me. She pushed me beyond my perceived limits.

One morning during team practice, I vividly remember going up for a jump shot and missing. While my teammates witnessed the surprising incident, my coach jerked the basketball from my hands and slammed it into my gut. I was taken by surprise and wondered, *Why did she do that?* With her bright-blue eyes, she stared at me without flinching, then exclaimed, "Don't miss it again!" As I began regaining my composure, I realized my breathing had been interrupted, and at that point, I certainly wanted to call timeout. With each passing year, her demands on me became stronger while eventually shaping me into a greater basketball player.

Much like my high school coach, God wants to be your life coach. He sees the winner in you, and He wants to bring it out. He created you with unlimited potential, and sometimes He uses others to challenge you to push harder in order to embrace the new frontier.

> What about you? Are the expectations on your
> life too great? Are the pressures too hard to
> handle? Unexpected circumstances may have
> knocked the breath out of you, leaving you weak
> and unable to go on. However, this is not the
> time to call timeout. Stand firm on God's truth,
> knowing that through Christ you can do it. You
> and Jesus together can win; therefore, go ahead
> and give it your best shot, and make it count.

Please remain strong while delighting in His wonderful promise. "With God all things are possible" (Matthew 19:26).

Your Reflections

I can do all things through Christ which strengtheneth me
(Philippians 4:13).

Get Set, Go!

◆ ◆ ◆

ON YOUR MARK, GET SET, GO! I can remember this phrase as a child when many of the neighborhood children would come together and compete in foot racing. The only thing that was rewarding was just having plain ole fun and pressing to not come in last place. Otherwise, you were considered the rotten egg. Although we did not compete to receive a particular prize, we all had the mind-set of winning.

The apostle Paul often compares the Christian life to running a race. He exhorts in Philippians 3:13–14,

> Brethren, I count not myself to have apprehended: but this one thing I do, forgetting those things which are behind, and reaching forth unto those things which are before, I press toward the mark for the prize of the high calling of God in Christ Jesus.

Paul is one of our greatest examples of running the Christian race. He ran it with faithfulness and endurance, with devotion and commitment. He suffered many afflictions, but he never lost sight of his purpose to press toward the prize of his calling. He was determined to make it to the finish line. Not once did he look back and replay the memories of his past. He stayed completely focused.

> At this very moment, you may be tempted to
> give up and stop running. Life can sometimes
> be hard and devastating, and the easiest thing
> to do is to quit and fall out of the race.

Be not discouraged, no matter what you are going through. Keep pressing so that you may finish the race. You must purpose in your heart that it is worth every effort to keep running. Your faith may be tested, but at the end of the finish line, you will be able to say, "I have fought a good fight, I have finished my course, I have kept the faith" (2 Timothy 4:7).

Your Reflections

_____

_____

_____

_____

_____

_____

_____

_____

_____

_____

_____

_____

_____

_____

_____

_____

_____

_____

_____

_____

_____

_____

_____

_____

_____

_____

_____

_____

Looking unto Jesus the author and finisher of our faith (Hebrews 12:2).

Go! Fight! Win!

♦ ♦ ♦

GO!-FIGHT!-WIN! The Saints are at it again. We're on the top and can't be stopped. Go! Fight! Win! When I hear this cheer/chant, I am reminded of the sweet memories of my high school basketball days. During one particular game, I vividly remember the overwhelming crowd; the gym was packed to the max.

The loud cheers and the applauding fans served as our reinforcement, encouraging us to play a little harder. We were two points up in an overtime with only thirteen seconds remaining and the ball was in the hands of our opponent. The petite five-foot-four guard headed toward the basket making every effort to tie the game for the second time around. My heart was beating out of control, but amazingly, she missed the shot. At the sound of the buzzer, the motivated crowd hit the floor with great excitement, shouting, "We won! We won!" I didn't think we would live through the pressure, but we made it and we received the victory!

In the same manner, we sometimes find ourselves living our lives under pressure. We allow ourselves to get too involved in life's circumstances instead of relying on God. Let's take a look at the example of the apostle Paul. He lived under constant pressure, yet he persevered. He makes it abundantly clear in 2 Corinthians 1:8–9. (NIV) "We were under great pressure, far beyond our ability to endure, so that we despaired of life itself ... But this happened that we might not rely on ourselves but on God."

My dear friend, stay in the game, and don't let the Enemy score on you. Guard him tightly with God's Word. Disregard all the bad calls, but listen closely to the words of encouragement from those that are cheering you onward. Encouragement is a powerful thing. It keeps you stronger, and it motivates you to keep up your momentum.

The Enemy can take his best shot, but you have full assurance that he will not win in the end because the Lord is on your side. Go! Fight! Win! You are at it again. You're on the top, and you can't be stopped. Go! Fight! Win!

Your Reflections

_____

_____

_____

_____

_____

_____

_____

_____

_____

_____

_____

_____

_____

_____

_____

_____

_____

_____

_____

_____

_____

_____

_____

_____

_____

_____

_____

Consider it a great joy ... whenever you experience various trials,
knowing that the testing of your faith produces endurance
(James 1:2-3). (CSB)

Mighty in God

♦♦♦

GIDEON WAS IN THE WINEPRESS SECRETLY threshing wheat in order to hide it from the Midianites. The angel of the Lord appeared unto him and said, "The Lord is with you, you mighty man of valor!" (Judges 6:12). I can hear Gideon asking, "Who, me?" Surely, the angel has made a mistake. However, that was not the case. Gideon, the weakest man in all of Israel, was chosen by God to accomplish a great task. Even though the odds appeared to be against him, it wasn't so with God. God had a simple but brilliant plan. He took Gideon's small army of warriors, divided them into three groups, and gave them victory over the Midianites, who consisted of more than 100,000 men. Isn't that amazing?

We are told in 1 Corinthians 1:27–29,

> But God hath chosen the foolish things of the world to confound the wise; and God hath chosen the weak things of the world to confound the things which are mighty; And base things of the world, and things which are despised, hath God chosen, yea, and things which are not, to bring to nought things that are: That no flesh should glory in his presence.

Although Gideon was fearful when he stepped to the position of the Israelite leader, he realized that his only way out was to trust God. Gideon reminds me of what Paul says to the Corinthians. "For when I am weak, then I am strong" (2 Corinthians 12:10).

> My dear friend, perhaps you are struggling with
> some weak areas in your life. Maybe they are
> holding you back. However, it's been said many
> times that man's extremity is God's opportunity.
> Therefore, be strong and let God work through you.

Just as God was with Gideon, He is with you also, you mighty person of valor. Let the hero within you rise up and know that you can't win the battle alone. But with God, it can be accomplished.

Your Reflections

_____

_____

_____

_____

_____

_____

_____

_____

_____

_____

_____

_____

_____

_____

_____

_____

_____

_____

_____

_____

_____

_____

_____

_____

_____

He giveth power to the faint; and to them that have no might he increaseth strength (Isaiah 40:29).

Giant Slayer

♦ ♦ ♦

DAVID SAID TO THE PHILISTINE,

Thou comest to me with a sword, and with a spear, and with a shield: but I come to thee in the name of the LORD of hosts, the God of the armies of Israel, whom thou hast defied. This day will the LORD deliver thee into mine hand; and I will smite thee, and take thine head from thee; and I will give the carcases of the host of the Philistines this day unto the fowls of the air, and to the wild beasts of the earth; that all the earth may know that there is a God in Israel. And all this assembly shall know that the LORD saveth not with sword and spear: for the battle is the LORD's, and he will give you into our hands. And it came to pass, when the Philistine arose, and came, and drew nigh to meet David, that David hastened, and ran toward the army to meet the Philistine. And David put his hand in his bag, and took thence a stone, and slang it, and smote the Philistine in his forehead, that the stone sunk into his forehead; and he fell upon his face to the earth. So David prevailed over the Philistine with a sling and

with a stone, and smote the Philistine, and slew him;
but there was no sword in the hand of David.
1 Samuel 17:45-50

Goliath, a giant who stood nine feet, nine inches tall and was strong and intimidating, brought fear upon King Saul and the Israelite soldiers. However, David, a young shepherd boy, was not afraid of the giant. He stepped into the valley and faced the giant head on. David did not have confidence in himself. His confidence was in the power of almighty God. In Psalm 23:4, we can hear the cry of David's voice. "Yea, though I walk through the valley of the shadow of death, I will fear no evil: for thou art with me; thy rod and thy staff they comfort me."

There are times in our lives when we are faced with circumstances that are far too big for us to handle. These are the times we must turn to God and rely solely upon His power and strength to deliver us. Don't look at how big your problem is. Instead, look at how big your God is. The same God that gave David victory over the giant will also give you victory over every giant that you are facing. David brought down the giant with one smooth rock; you too can bring down your giant with a rock, and that rock is Jesus.

I want to encourage you to, "Be strong in the Lord and in the power of His might" (Ephesians 6:10). Your victory over spiritual forces does not come by physical strength or carnal weapons. Your victory comes by putting on the spiritual weapons of God. Then you are able to walk in faith, knowing that your giants have been taken down.

Your Reflections

_____
_____
_____
_____
_____
_____
_____
_____
_____
_____
_____
_____
_____
_____
_____
_____
_____
_____
_____
_____
_____
_____
_____
_____
_____

Put on the whole armour of God, that ye may be able to stand against the wiles of the devil (Ephesians 6:11).

The Waiting Room

◆◆◆

"WHAT'S TAKING SO LONG?" I asked while sitting in the ER waiting room at UAMS Hospital. After sitting there for nearly seven hours, I began to get impatient. It seemed like everything was put on hold and I had been forgotten. I have never been good at waiting, but through the process of my life, there were times when I had no choice but to wait on God.

At some point in our lives, we all have prayed and waited on God for the results. Sometimes, our prayers are answered right away, and there are times when God allows us to go through a season of waiting before we actually see the full manifestation. In either case, we still have to trust God for the answer. He knows what is best for us, even when we can't see the best.

The waiting room has its purpose. It is just another process we go through in order to get the needed results. It develops our character, it strengthens our faith, and it carries us to the place that God desires for us. Our strength is renewed, and then we are able to soar above all of our troubles.

> If by chance you are in the waiting room, be
> certain that God is already working on your
> behalf. There is no need to become weary or lose

125

heart. Get rid of all anxieties and concerns, and
place them in the hands of your heavenly Father.

In Genesis 15:1-2, God tells Abraham, "I am thy shield, and thy exceeding great reward." Abraham asked, "What wilt thou give me, seeing I go childless?" God affirmed His promise to Abraham. Abraham and Sarah spent more than twenty years in the waiting room. At the appointed time, God blessed them with the promised son. God's timing is the best timing. He has so many wonderful things in store for us if we just trust Him and wait.

Your Reflections

_____

_____

_____

_____

_____

_____

_____

_____

_____

_____

_____

_____

_____

_____

_____

_____

_____

_____

_____

_____

_____

_____

_____

_____

_____

*But they that wait upon the L*ORD *shall renew their strength; they shall mount up with wings as eagles; they shall run, and not be weary; and they shall walk, and not faint (Isaiah 40:31).*

It's Worth the Wait

♦ ♦ ♦

YOU PRAY, AND NOTHING HAPPENS. YOU PRAY SOME MORE, and still nothing happens. You step it up another notch, yet your circumstances remain the same. I don't know about you, but there have been times when I have become emotionally exhausted from praying the same prayer over and over again. And when things don't develop at the pace I want them to, I begin to wonder if something is wrong with my communication. "Hello, God. Can you hear me? I have a problem that needs your immediate attention." This is exactly how most of us feel when we don't get our prayers answered right away. We grow impatient, and when the waiting process takes a toll on us, we become downright miserable. We want what we want, and we want it right now.

However, God doesn't always give us the lowdown on how and when He is going to answer our prayers. We just have to have faith and accept the truth that He has perfect timing and He knows what's best for us.

I know you too have had your own personal trial with waiting. But in the long run, it will work out better on your behalf if you just hold strong instead of trying to fix it yourself. Even though you can't see it, God is at work in your life. He suddenly shows up, letting you know that He hears your prayers, and ultimately He hasn't forgotten you.

Having patience can be tough sometimes. But regardless of how hard it gets, continue hoping, believing, and trusting that God has worked everything out. "And we know that all things work together for good to them that love God, to them who are the called according to his purpose" (Romans 8:28).

Your Reflections

_____

_____

_____

_____

_____

_____

_____

_____

_____

_____

_____

_____

_____

_____

_____

_____

_____

_____

_____

_____

_____

_____

_____

_____

_____

_____

_____

For the LORD is a God of judgment: blessed are all they that wait for him (Isaiah 30:18).

The Road of Difficulty

◆◆◆

GOD IS JUST THAT WONDERFUL! He always keep His promises. During the past eleven months of my life, my journey has been a difficult one. I am not going to patronize you by telling you that it has been easy. Life is not always easy, and it can make a sudden U-turn that will lunge you in a direction that you never intended. I will not lavish you with deception by making you think that I have been a superwoman of faith. Ultimately, I have not. I have strictly relied on my faith in God. Otherwise, I would have hit the ground and crumbled. After suffering the loss of someone that was so special to me, it appeared that my life was wrecked and I had little hope of survival. My vehicle was my sanctuary. If it could have held the tears that were shed, it would be under water right now. Yet God has been my stronghold through it all, and He remained faithful to His promise.

I often wondered, *Will my life return to normal?"* However, it will never be normal like before, but there is grace in finding a new normal. My new normal has allowed me to live again and accept the plans that He has for me.

To those of you who have and are traveling the road of difficulty, I want to encourage you to remain steadfast. You have heard many times, "When the going gets tough, the tough gets going." But I say, "When the going gets tough, the tough hang in there and persevere." I know that is easier said than done, but trust me: I know this from experience.

James 1:12 (NIV) reminds us, "Blessed is the man who perseveres under trial, because when he has stood the test, he will receive the crown of life that God has promised to those who love him."

You too will make it through this ordeal. Just get through today, and I promise you tomorrow will bring new opportunities and a whole new perspective on life.

Your Reflections

_____

_____

_____

_____

_____

_____

_____

_____

_____

_____

_____

_____

_____

_____

_____

_____

_____

_____

_____

_____

_____

_____

_____

_____

_____

Thy word is a lamp unto my feet, and a light unto my path
(Psalm 119:105).

The Road Less Traveled

♦ ♦ ♦

WOULDN'T IT BE WONDERFUL IF WE COULD LOOK through a telescope of time and see our life in full detail, knowing that the outcome of every situation will have a happy ending? Unfortunately, that is certainly not how life is. Life is a journey of faith, and we must rely on God every step of the way, even though we do not know how it will turn out or where we will end up.

We are told in Genesis 12:1 that the Lord said to Abram, "Get thee out of thy country!" Abram went out and traveled to a foreign country, not knowing what to expect. He did not know where he was going, and he certainly didn't have the luxury of carrying along a road map or a turn-by-turn navigation system. Abram's faith was tested, but he relied on God's Word. "I am with you and will watch over you wherever you go, and I will bring you back to this land. I will not leave you until I have done what I have promised you" (Genesis 28.15). (NIV)

My journey of faith was definitely tested when I was suddenly thrust into a new direction of life. I was baffled with the unfamiliar path while struggling with the fact that I didn't know where I would end up. I wasted many hours trying to decipher the details of my life, when God only wanted me to trust Him as He led the way.

It's much easier to trust God when we can see where we are headed, but God doesn't always show us that. Sometimes, all we get is the next step. In Psalm 37:23, David reminds us that "The steps of a good man are ordered by the Lord, and He delighteth in his way."

Perhaps your life has taken a different turn. And as much as you would like, you would prefer to take the easy road, one that is familiar, comfortable, and convenient. The easy road can sometimes appear to take you where you want to go. Don't be surprised if He sends you down the road less traveled. However, the road less traveled is often the one that holds the greatest promise. "Go!" He's with you.

Your Reflections

_____

_____

_____

_____

_____

_____

_____

_____

_____

_____

_____

_____

_____

_____

_____

_____

_____

_____

_____

_____

_____

_____

_____

_____

And the LORD, he it is that doth go before thee (Deuteronomy 31:8).

Standing at the Crossroads

◆◆◆

LIFE IS FULL OF UNEXPECTED TWISTS AND TURNS. One day everything seems to be going according to plans while working toward your life-long dreams. And then, like a lightning bolt out of the blue, you are hit with the biggest blow of your life that knocks you off course. Suddenly, you find yourself standing at the crossroads of life, pondering, *Where will I go from here? Should I go left, or should I go right?*

In my case, I certainly know what it feels like to be knocked off your path and have your dreams demolished in an instant. Unexpectedly, I was facing the world of the unknown and I had no idea where I would end up. Standing within the four walls of my laundry room, helpless, feeling stranded as though someone had dropped me off along the roadside, I asked myself, "Where will I go from here? Will I live through this ordeal, or will I lie down and die?" After working through this issue in my mind, I made a conscious decision to live and navigate through the obstacles and setbacks that were placed on my path.

Would I have chosen this path? Absolutely not! But I am convinced that God is very much involved in what is transpiring. Therefore, I must remain faithful to Him through every test and trial. Foremost, it is up to me to stand strong through the process while He purifies and molds me into becoming the person that He desires me to be. Despite aspirations and dreams, our lives do not always turn out as planned. The writer of Proverbs 19:21 (NIV) records, "Many are the plans in a man's heart, but it is the Lord's purpose that prevails."

> The path that you are on may not make sense
> or seem remotely logical. But God has led you
> where you are for a reason. His plans are always
> the right plans because He has distinct vision
> that can see far greater ahead than you can.

The voice of Jeremiah echoes in 29:11. (NIV) "For I know the plans I have for you, declares the LORD, plans to prosper you and not to harm you, plans to give you hope and a future."

Your Reflections

_____

_____

_____

_____

_____

_____

_____

_____

_____

_____

_____

_____

_____

_____

_____

_____

_____

_____

_____

_____

_____

_____

_____

_____

_____

For My thoughts are not your thoughts, neither are your ways my ways, saith the Lord (Isaiah 55:8).

The Rearview Mirror

♦♦♦

PUTTING FORTH EVERY EFFORT TO LOOK FORWARD, I still find myself looking through the rearview mirror, staring at glimpses of my past, which I cannot let go. Most people tend to struggle with letting go of what they are familiar with because the past is what everyone knows. Although God understands our struggles, He desires for us to move forward and embrace the new. Isaiah 43:18–19 tells us, "Remember ye not the former things, neither consider the things of old. Behold, I will do a new thing; now it shall spring forth; shall ye not know it? I will even make a way in the wilderness, and rivers in the desert."

If you are running in a race, it is almost impossible to look behind and continue running with the same pace and momentum as you would looking forward. Likewise, it's impossible for us to move forward in life when we are constantly dwelling on our past experiences. Our past hinders our progress and keeps us from reaching our full potential. It can be a delay and a distraction to our future promises.

In Philippians 3:13 (MSG), the apostle Paul boldly declares,

> I'm not saying that I have this all together, that I have it made. But I am well on my way, reaching out for

Christ, who has so wondrously reached out for me. Friends, don't get me wrong: By no means do I count myself an expert in all of this, but I've got my eye on the goal, where God is beckoning us onward—to Jesus. I'm off and running, and I'm not turning back.

Since our goal is in Christ Jesus, we can let go of our past and look forward to what God will help us become and achieve.

If you are in a place where you're not able to see a future for yourself, then there is a good chance you are locked in the past. My dear friend, you must turn your focus on the road ahead, because the past you cannot change. You cannot relive it; you cannot replay it. You must accept the change and start moving toward the new assignment that God has prepared for you.

> You may be hurting at this very moment, you may
> be weak and struggling, but your past will not defeat
> you. God's grace will enable you to rise up and move
> forward, way beyond what you can ever imagine.

The next time you are tempted to look through your rearview mirror, remind yourself that God has greater things waiting for you ahead.

Your Reflections

_____

_____

_____

_____

_____

_____

_____

_____

_____

_____

_____

_____

_____

_____

_____

_____

_____

_____

_____

_____

_____

_____

_____

Brethren, I count not myself to have apprehended: but this one thing I do, forgetting those things which are behind, and reaching forth unto those things which are before (Philippians 3:13).

Perpetual Praise

◆ ◆ ◆

THE BIBLE REVEALS TO US THAT DAVID WAS A MAN after God's own heart. He loved God with his whole heart, and oftentimes he had to encourage himself in the Lord by praising Him. In Psalm 34, he writes,

> I will bless the LORD at all times: his praise shall continually be in my mouth. My soul shall make her boast in the LORD: the humble shall hear thereof, and be glad. O magnify the LORD with me, and let us exalt his name together.

One of the most interesting things about this passage is that David wrote this song of praise right in the middle of adversity. He set a good example by encouraging us that, regardless of what our circumstances are, continuous praise should flow from our lips. "But thou art holy, O thou that inhabitest the praises of Israel" (Psalm 22:3).

There are times in my life when I am tempted to say, "Woe is me." Instead, I choose to be like David. I will praise God no matter what I am going through. I will praise at all times.

Perhaps you are feeling discouraged. Just like David encouraged himself in the Lord, you must do the same. So lift your hands and give God adoration for who He is. "O give thanks unto the LORD, for he is good: for his mercy endureth for ever" (Psalm 107:1).

Your Reflections

_____

_____

_____

_____

_____

_____

_____

_____

_____

_____

_____

_____

_____

_____

_____

_____

_____

_____

_____

_____

_____

_____

_____

_____

_____

While I live will I praise the LORD: I will sing praises unto my God while I have any being (Psalm 146:2).

At Midnight

♦ ♦ ♦

"AND AT MIDNIGHT PAUL AND SILAS PRAYED, and sang praises unto God: and the prisoners heard them. And suddenly there was a great earthquake, so that the foundations of the prison were shaken: and immediately all the doors were opened, and every one's chains were loosed" (Act 16:25–26).

While Paul and Silas were going throughout the city of Philippi, doing the will of God, they were challenged by a multitude who falsely accused them of starting trouble in their city. You know the story. Paul and Silas were stripped of their clothing, beaten, and thrown in the uttermost part of prison. I would expect that being in prison is not a place where one would find joy, and certainly one wouldn't have the best attitude after being beaten half to death. But Paul and Silas showed a great example of how to respond to troubles.

These two men, full of the Holy Spirit, could have complained and blamed God for being attacked for doing His work. Instead, they found peace in prison while being chained up and suffering from their open wounds. As they sang praises to God, God intervened on their behalf by allowing an earthquake to come and shake loose the prison walls.

Are you in the midnight hour where things are
the darkest and you can't see your way out? Are
you in an unpleasant place where bonds have
been placed on your life? Perhaps the Enemy has
stripped you of your dignity, finances, health,
job, or even a relationship. Regardless of your
situation, stand up boldly and start praising God.

It's easy to praise God when everything is going right. But your true character can only be revealed when you are able to praise Him in the midst of your circumstances. As you continue in your praise to Him, you can be certain that He will act on your behalf, tearing down the walls that have been built around you. Never doubt God in your midnight hour.

"You give us victory over our enemies, you put our adversaries to shame" (Psalm 44:7). (NIV)

Your Reflections

_____

_____

_____

_____

_____

_____

_____

_____

_____

_____

_____

_____

_____

_____

_____

_____

_____

_____

_____

_____

_____

_____

_____

I will greatly praise the LORD with my mouth; yea, I will praise him among the multitude (Psalm 109:30).

Hello, God, It's Me Again

◆◆◆

KING JEHOSHAPHAT WAS FACING A SERIOUS PROBLEM. A great multitude of his enemy was preparing themselves for battle against him and his people. "What's my next step?" he asked himself. Ultimately, he turned to God once more and unashamedly poured out his heart. "Hello, God, it's me again: King Jehoshaphat. I have another problem, and I need your help." He prayed, "I am a weak man, and I don't have the strength or resources to overcome the enemy."

After his devotion, the king gathered the people and they began offering praises to God. "Praise the Lord; for His mercy endures forever" (2 Chronicles 20:21). It has been said many times that a man's praise is the gateway to experiencing God's blessing.

Now let me tell you how the story ended. The praises of King Jehoshaphat and the people brought so much confusion in the camp of the enemy that they turned on one another. And as a result, the battle was won and the king gathered all the silver, gold, and jewels.

So what did I learn from the king's story? First and foremost, I need to go immediately to God when I am in trouble; I need to spend time with Him in prayer and seek His guidance. Even before I see the victory, I need to praise Him.

> What about you, my friend? Are you in need of
> God's help? Don't waste another minute trying to
> figure out a solution to your problem. Just pour out
> your heart freely to Him, your one and only refuge.

Be encouraged as you meditate on the following Scripture: "God is our refuge and strength, a very present help in trouble" (Psalm 46:1).

Your Reflections

_____

_____

_____

_____

_____

_____

_____

_____

_____

_____

_____

_____

_____

_____

_____

_____

_____

_____

_____

_____

_____

_____

_____

_____

_____

I will extol thee, O Lord; for thou hast lifted me up, and hast not made my foes to rejoice over me. O Lord my God, I cried unto thee, and thou hast healed me (Psalm 30:1-2).

Light of the World

◆ ◆ ◆

AS I WAS ENTERING MY HOME one afternoon, there lay a taper candle on the doorsteps. Unfortunately, the candle had been stepped on and broken. The candle lay there for several days before being picked up. There is more to be said, but I love the fact that even though the candle was broken, it could still serve its main purpose. And that is to give light.

Even as Christians, sometimes our unfortunate experiences leave us feeling broken. We feel that we have no purpose in God's kingdom. My friend, I have good news for you. God can still use you regardless of what state your circumstance may have left you in. Please be encouraged by reading Matthew 5:14–15. (NKJV)

> You are the light of the world. A city that is set on a hill cannot be hidden. Nor do they light a lamp and put it under a basket, but on a lampstand, and it gives light to all who are in the house.

One of the greatest demonstration of God's love throughout Scriptures is how He salvaged broken lives. He went on to use these people in many great ways. David reminds us in Psalm

34:18, (NIV) "The Lord is close to the brokenhearted and saves those who are crushed in spirit."

Brokenness can be a stepping-stone. It can be another opportunity for God to show Himself powerful through you. Don't give up or give in. Stand tall like the taper candle and let your light shine. Someone needs to see your light today.

Your Reflections

_____

_____

_____

_____

_____

_____

_____

_____

_____

_____

_____

_____

_____

_____

_____

_____

_____

_____

_____

_____

_____

_____

_____

*For God, who commanded the light to shine out of darkness, hath
shined in our hearts, to give the light of the knowledge of the glory of
God in the face of Jesus Christ (2 Corinthians 4:6).*

Child of Destiny

♦♦♦

HAVE YOU BEEN SEARCHING DEEP DOWN TRYING TO DISCOVER what your purpose is in life? Do you find fulfillment and peace with the direction that your life is taking? Believe it or not, most Christians struggle with defining their God-given purpose. You may ask, "Where do I start?" It all starts with God. It is only in Him that you discover who you are and what you were put on this planet to do. You were made by Him and for Him. His purpose is always revealed through mankind.

We are told that God had great purpose for the children of Israel to lead them out of Egypt to the Promised Land. Some scholars say that what was meant to be an eleven-day journey turned into forty years of wandering in the wilderness. This generation of Israelites did not make it to their destiny. They did not live out their purpose that God had divinely set for them.

It's God's desire that you walk in your destiny and enjoy the purpose of your creation. Jeremiah 1:5 states, "Before I formed you in the belly I knew thee; and before thou camest forth out of the womb I sanctified thee, and I ordained thee a prophet unto the nations." He created you because He appointed you for something special. When you were conceived, He was there. When you were born, He was there, and it pleases Him that His will is accomplished through you. You were not an afterthought, or a mistake. God does not make mistakes. Everything He made, He made intentionally.

> God wants to take you out of the wandering
> zone and place you on the path to your destiny.
> As you walk in God's plan for your life, you will
> become passionate for what you do for Him;
> you will become great at what you do for Him.
> Most of all, you will please Him and make Him
> proud that you are a part of His creation.

But you are the ones chosen by God, chosen for the high calling of priestly work, chosen to be a holy people, God's instruments to do His work and speak out for Him, to tell others of the night and day difference He made for you—from nothing to something, from rejected to accepted.
1 Peter 2:9–10 (MSG)

Your Reflections

_____

_____

_____

_____

_____

_____

_____

_____

_____

_____

_____

_____

_____

_____

_____

_____

_____

_____

_____

_____

_____

_____

_____

_____

_____

For thou art an holy people unto the LORD thy God: the LORD thy God hath chosen thee to be a special people unto himself, above all people that are upon the face of the earth (Deuteronomy 7:6).

You Are His Masterpiece

♦ ♦ ♦

"THEN I WENT DOWN TO THE POTTER'S HOUSE, and, behold, he wrought a work on the wheels. And the vessel that he made of clay was marred in the hand of the potter: so he made it again another vessel, as seemed good to the potter to make it" (Jeremiah 18:3–4).

It's always a pleasure to visit Eureka Springs, Arkansas, and enjoy all of the attractions they have to offer. However, on one occasion, I was very blessed while visiting the potter's house and personally witnessed the works of the potter's hand. It was amazing how he was able to take formless clay and make beautiful earthen vessels of many shapes and sizes. But what's more amazing is that God physically shaped Adam from the dust of the earth and breathed into him the breath of life, and he became a living being. Likewise, we are formed from clay. Better yet, He wants to shape and mold us in the image of His very own son, Jesus Christ.

Ephesians 2:10 tells us that we are His workmanship, created in Christ Jesus. However, becoming the masterpiece that He desires, He will begin shaping us for better things. He is the potter; we are the clay. To get us into better shape may require pummeling, chiseling, and painful molding. It may also require a fiery trial in the oven of testing. But we can be sure that our master potter knows what is necessary for us to become the vessel for His use. With all of our imperfections and flaws, he doesn't throw us aside and give up on us. He patiently works with us, and He carefully watches over us.

Be encouraged. You are a divine work of art, a masterpiece of God, and "He who began a good work in you will carry it on to completion until the day of Jesus Christ" (Philippians 1:6). (NIV)

Your Reflections

_____
_____
_____
_____
_____
_____
_____
_____
_____
_____
_____
_____
_____
_____
_____
_____
_____
_____
_____
_____
_____
_____
_____
_____

_Take away the dross from the silver, and there shall come forth a vessel
for the finer (Proverbs 25:4)._

Backside of the Desert

♦♦♦

"AND THE ANGEL OF THE LORD APPEARED TO HIM in a flame of fire out the midst of a bush: and he looked, and, behold, the bush burned with fire, yet the bush was not consumed" (Exodus 3:2).

Running for his life, some forty years later, Moses ended up on the backside of the desert tending sheep for his father-in-law, Jethro. On just any ordinary day in the desert, it was common to witness a bush burning, which lasted only a few seconds, leaving a smoldering pile of ashes. But this bush was different. It kept burning and burning.

The burning bush captivated Moses' attention. Therefore, he had to explore farther to see what was happening. As he began to move closer, the voice of God emitted from the bush, commanding him to not come any closer. At this point, I can imagine Moses being a bit scared and confused, but he soon realized that this experience was a mere encounter with God. This encounter, however, was preparation for Moses to be taken to the next phase of his life.

Perhaps your journey has taken you to the backside of the desert, causing you to feel a sense of discouragement. The key is to remember that desert experiences are a part of life and you shall be abundantly rewarded if you remain steadfast in your faith.

I have learned that some of life's hard-earned lessons can come out of a place of desolation and isolation. It is most likely during these times He is able to capture our attention. He doesn't just get our attention and leave us wandering. He gets our attention so we can be led into greater and higher plains.

Like Moses, God can use you to do great and mighty things for His kingdom. No distance or time can keep you away from Him. When you have been chosen by God and when He gets ready to use you for His purpose, He will find you wherever you are. We are reminded in Proverbs 5:21, "For the ways of man are before the eyes of the LORD, and He pondereth all his goings."

Your Reflections

_____

_____

_____

_____

_____

_____

_____

_____

_____

_____

_____

_____

_____

_____

_____

_____

_____

_____

_____

_____

_____

_____

_____

_____

_____

_____

He found him in a desert land, and in the waste howling wilderness; he led him about, he instructed him, he kept him as the apple of his eye (Deuteronomy 32:10).

Additional Scriptures for Comfort and Encouragement

Deuteronomy 31:6: "Be strong and of a good courage, fear not, nor be afraid of them: for the LORD thy God, he it is that doth go with thee; he will not fail thee, nor forsake thee."

Isaiah 41:10: "Fear thou not; for I am with thee: be not dismayed; for I am thy God: I will strengthen thee; yea, I will help thee; yea, I will uphold thee with the right hand of my righteousness."

Zephaniah 3:17: "The LORD thy God in the midst of thee is mighty; he will save, he will rejoice over thee with joy; he will rest in his love, he will joy over thee with singing."

1 Corinthians 10:13: "There hath no temptation taken you but such as is common to man: but God is faithful, who will not suffer you to be tempted above that ye are able; but will with the temptation also make a way to escape, that ye may be able to bear it."

2 Corinthians 4:16–18: "For which cause we faint not; but though our outward man perish, yet the inward man is renewed day by day. For our light affliction, which is but for a moment, worketh for us a far more exceeding and eternal weight of glory; While we look not at the things which are seen, but at the things which are not seen: for the things which are seen are temporal; but the things which are not seen are eternal."

Deuteronomy 31:8: "And the LORD, he it is that doth go before thee; he will be with thee, he will not fail thee, neither forsake thee: fear not, neither be dismayed."

Psalm 9:9-10 "The LORD also will be a refuge for the oppressed, a refuge in times of trouble. And they that know thy name will put their trust in thee: for thou, LORD, hast not forsaken them that seek thee."

Psalm 23:4: "Yea, though I walk through the valley of the shadow of death, I will fear no evil: for thou art with me; thy rod and thy staff they comfort me."

Psalm 55:22: "Cast thy burden upon the LORD, and he shall sustain thee: he shall never suffer the righteous to be moved."

Matthew 11:28–29: "Come unto me, all ye that labour and are heavy laden, and I will give you rest. Take my yoke upon you, and learn of me; for I am meek and lowly in heart: and ye shall find rest unto your souls."

John 14:27: "Peace I leave with you, my peace I give unto you: not as the world giveth, give I unto you. Let not your heart be troubled, neither let it be afraid."

John 16:33: "These things I have spoken unto you, that in me ye might have peace. In the world ye shall have tribulation: but be of good cheer; I have overcome the world."

Romans 8:6: "For to be carnally minded is death; but to be spiritually minded is life and peace."

Philippians 4:6–7: "Be careful for nothing; but in every thing by prayer and supplication with thanksgiving let your requests be made known unto God. And the peace of God, which passeth all understanding, shall keep your hearts and minds through Christ Jesus."

Colossians 3:15: "And let the peace of God rule in your hearts, to the which also ye are called in one body; and be ye thankful."

Titus 3:7: "That being justified by his grace, we should be made heirs according to the hope of eternal life."

1 Corinthians 15:19: "If in Christ we have hope in this life only, we are of all people most to be pitied."

Psalm 46:10-11: "Be still, and know that I am God: I will be exalted among the heathen, I will be exalted in the earth. The Lord of hosts is with us; the God of Jacob is our refuge. Selah."

1 Peter 1:3-4: "Blessed be the God and Father of our Lord Jesus Christ, which according to his abundant mercy hath begotten us again unto a lively hope by the resurrection of Jesus Christ from the dead. To an inheritance incorruptible, and undefiled, and that fadeth not away, reserved in heaven for you."

Romans 5:2–5: "By whom also we have access by faith into this grace wherein we stand, and rejoice in hope of the glory of God. And not only so, but we glory in tribulations also: knowing that tribulation worketh patience; And patience, experience; and experience, hope: And hope maketh not ashamed; because the love of God is shed abroad in our hearts by the Holy Ghost which is given unto us."

Romans 8:24–25: "For we are saved by hope: but hope that is seen is not hope: for what a man seeth, why doth he yet hope for? But if we hope for that we see not, then do we with patience wait for it."

Romans 12:12: "Rejoicing in hope; patient in tribulation; continuing instant in prayer;"

Romans 15:4: "For whatsoever things were written aforetime were written for our learning, that we through patience and comfort of the scriptures might have hope."

Romans 15:13: "Now the God of hope fill you with all joy and peace in believing, that ye may abound in hope, through the power of the Holy Ghost."

Numbers 23:19: "God is not a man, that he should lie; neither the son of man, that he should repent: hath he said, and shall he not do it? or hath he spoken, and shall he not make it good?"

Psalm 23:1-3: "The LORD is my shepherd; I shall not want. He maketh me to lie down in green pastures: he leadeth me beside the still waters. He restoreth my soul: he leadeth me in the paths of righteousness for his name's sake."

John 4:13–14: "Jesus answered and said unto her, Whosoever drinketh of this water shall thirst again: But whosoever drinketh of the water that I shall give him shall never thirst; but the water that I shall give him shall be in him a well of water springing up into everlasting life."

Hebrews 11:1: "Now faith is the substance of things hoped for, the evidence of things not seen."

Your Reflections

_____

_____

_____

_____

_____

_____

_____

_____

_____

_____

_____

_____

_____

_____

_____

_____

_____

_____

_____

_____

_____

_____

_____

_____

_____

_____

_____

_____

_____

_____

_____

_____

_____

_____

_____

_____

_____

_____

_____

_____

_____

_____

_____

_____

_____

_____

_____

_____

_____

_____

_____

_____

_____

_____

_____

_____

_____

But my God shall supply all your need according to his riches in glory by Christ Jesus (Philippians 4:19).

About the Author

Carolyn Crow continues in the pursuit of helping people find their way to a better life. A native of Gurdon, Arkansas, she made her commitment to Christ as a teenager, and since then, she has had a heart for loving God and serving people.

She is a gifted communicator, musician, songwriter, and Bible teacher who received her Bible training from Rhema Bible College in Tulsa, Oklahoma, and World Harvest Bible College of Columbus, Ohio. She speaks at Christian women conferences with her unique style, while paving a pathway of encouragement and hope to people from all walks of life. She resides in Arkadelphia, Arkansas.

CPSIA information can be obtained at www.ICGtesting.com
Printed in the USA
LVOW13s0301080714

393317LV00001B/245/P